TOP RUNNING TIPS

TOP RUNNING TIPS

151 Ways To Improve Your Running –
Easy Strategies You Can Use Right Now!

Interior pages design: Lazar Kackarovski

Printed by CreateSpace, an Amazon.com Company
Available from Amazon.com, CreateSpace.com, and other retail outlets

TOP RUNNING TIPS

151 WAYS TO IMPROVE YOUR RUNNING
EASY STRATEGIES YOU CAN USE RIGHT NOW!

JAGO HOLMES

TABLE OF **CONTENTS**

1 CHAPTER — TIPS FOR **BEGINNERS**

1. BOOK YOUR FIRST RACE

If you've decided that you're going to start running, then you'll need a little extra motivation at times. In the beginning, if your training is right, you can expect to make very good progress indeed, but there will still be times when life gets in the way... you've got to work late, the kids need you after school or you have errands to run etc.

This is when you'll need the motivation to get that extra run in- either later the same evening or at some other time that week. Miss too many training sessions and your fitness levels will quickly start to deteriorate. By booking a race in advance, you have a set date to work towards and the extra motivation and drive to put into your running.

2. GET YOURSELF A RUNNING BUDDY

There are a few reasons why running with someone else is a great idea, especially to get started. Firstly, the person you run with will give you extra support and motivation. You'll be accountable to someone else other than yourself and will have made arrangements with another person. This way you're far more likely to make it to your running sessions when you're supposed to.

If your running buddy is another beginner, you'll also be able to share the journey together which is a very supportive thing to do. If that person is already a good runner or even more experienced than you, then they'll be able to help you to set the pace and move forwards with your fitness as efficiently as possible.

A running buddy also provides one other very important function. They are your own personal safety officer. They'll look out for you and you them- just in case you get into any sticky situations.

3. EVERY RUN WON'T BE YOUR FINEST

Don't forget, even following the best running program possible, that your body will need to be coaxed and encouraged to change. You won't physically be able to run further or faster every time you run. Sure, that's the goal- especially in the early days- but there will be days when you don't run your best. Simply accept that fact and finish your run. Sometimes any run is better than no run at all.

There are many reasons why you won't be able to perform your best. Illness, tiredness, injury, poor diet, aching muscles etc. are all reasons that can very easily affect your performance.

4. KEEP A RUNNING JOURNAL

Here is a good one you can print out and use yourself (you'll have to sign up for the newsletter to get the download details for the journal, but it's well worth it) – *Get Your Free Printable Running Journal Here*

Your journal should include the date, time, route and conditions of your run. Your heart rate either during or on completion is always an interesting statistic you can monitor as well as the foods you eat before you run. What you're aiming for is to create a motivational tool to keep you on track when you don't feel like running.

5. JUST RUN

Don't sit down and think about your run too much before you go, especially if you're not really looking forward to doing it. Over-thinking your running can easily make you dread your sessions. Simply decide in advance when and where you'll run and when the time arrives, get your kit on and go out and do it. You won't get any better at it until you run on a regular basis.

6. DON'T KILL IT BEFORE YOU EVEN GET STARTED

Beginners often fall into this common trap. They're so motivated and determined at the start that they do too much, too soon. They want to run whenever they can because they start to see and feel the benefits of what they're doing.

Unfortunately the human body doesn't usually respond too well to overload like this and instead needs to be coaxed and encouraged into change. Sometimes it's better to hold yourself back until you've got used to the impact on the joints and the stress on the muscles that running incurs. Ignoring this simple advice often leads to progress stopping injuries.

In the beginning you don't want to run more than 2 or 3 times a week - at the most.

7. BE YOUR OWN MOTIVATIONAL SPEAKER

We all have voices in our heads telling us to do one thing or another all day long, but unfortunately, they are rarely positive. So why not use that voice to be your own personal trainer and motivational coach?

Build yourself up before you run and keep chipping away with positive encouragement along the way. Don't use words like 'can't do, won't do, never, I need to stop etc.' Be in charge, accept that you won't be able to keep running endlessly and instead give yourself permission to stop when you need to.

8. SET MINI TARGETS NOT LIFETIME AMBITIONS!

In the early days of your running regime, even the shortest of runs may seem quite a daunting prospect - especially if your fitness levels are low to begin with. Instead of expecting too much, break down your training runs into blocks of time or set distances that you can strive to reach.

When you've built up the fitness levels to achieve these targets then you'll need to reset your goals. If you set yourself a large challenge such as running a half marathon for example and break it down into smaller, more manageable chunks, then you'll be less daunted by it and far more likely to go out and achieve it.

9. RUN YOUR OWN RACE

Even if you're running on your own there is always a tendency to seek out verification that you are doing things correctly. This is natural and a perfectly acceptable thing to do. However, most of the time, this will come with some other type of guidance in terms of how far you should run and what pace you ought to run at.

In the beginning, it really doesn't matter what speed you go at or how far you run. Just concentrate on what you're doing and how you're improving against yourself. Using a running log is a great way of doing this.

If you do have a training partner, then don't try to run at their pace. If you're not fit enough to keep up, you'll quickly burn out. If you are fitter than they are, then you'll gradually stop making progress until their fitness level is similar to yours.

10. WARM UP PROPERLY BEFORE YOU START

Don't worry, this doesn't mean spending half an hour doing some complicated stretching and mobilising routine. For beginners, a good warm up is simply spending five minutes gently warming up the heart, lungs and muscles. The easiest way to do this is by walking slowly for a minute, then building up to a power walk for three minutes, then very gentle jogging for a further minute.

At this point the muscles will have warmed up a little and you'll be ready to do some gentle roadside stretches for your calves, hamstrings, hip flexors, quads and glutes. Then you're ready for the off...

11. DON'T DO IT IF YOU DON'T ENJOY IT

Whatever you think that running is going to do for you... be it to give you more energy, help you to get fitter or lose weight – which are just a few benefits of running- it won't work if you don't do it regularly. So, if you hate running, then don't force yourself to do it, instead find something else that you enjoy doing and can actually look forward to.

12. DON'T SET OFF LIKE A BULL AT A GATE

Another one of the biggest mistakes all newbie's make when starting to run is setting off too fast. The problem with doing this is that you will get so tired and drained after the first burst of effort that you have you nothing left to give afterwards. Alternatively, you can push yourself so far that you feel sick, dizzy, or light-headed and then have to stop.

There are a few problems with following this approach...

a) Firstly, it will be very uncomfortable, even painful to do, so it won't be remotely enjoyable
b) Secondly, because your experience of running is one of pain and discomfort, you naturally won't want to do it again anytime soon.
c) Lastly, running as hard as you can for a few minutes (or seconds!) then stopping isn't long enough to build any strength or real endurance into the legs or cardiovascular system.

13. DON'T RELY ON WILLPOWER ALONE

Everyone needs their fair share of willpower at some time or another when it comes to exercise and running is no different.

You have to be able to differentiate between times when you can't be bothered and times when you actually need to rest. You'll have to listen to your body and not your heart here. So, if you're feeling under the weather or are particularly tired, you might get more benefit by resting instead of pushing your body regardless.

Willpower is a really good thing to have, but maturity will help you to make the best decisions when it comes to whether you should or shouldn't exercise.

14. TIE YOUR SHOELACES PROPERLY

Every time you stop to re-tie your shoelaces, you get out of your rhythm and might struggle to get back on track. Tie your shoes with a double knot and make sure they're tied tightly. Many running accidents and injuries are caused by tripping over loose shoelaces or running in poorly fitting running shoes.

15. JOIN A RUNNING CLUB

If you're a complete beginner, one of the best options for you is to join a running club. Make sure that they have a beginner's group that you can run with at first as you don't want to feel slower than everyone else. A starter group like this will have many other runners at the same level of fitness and you'll all be going through the same emotions and making the journey together. It gives you a great support network and a new social life – which is always a great idea when it is based around an activity or sport.

16. START YOUR OWN RUNNING CLUB

If the thought of running with a bunch of complete strangers fills you with dread, then don't do it. Instead, why not look into creating your own running group? You can enlist family members, friends, neighbours, work colleagues etc. If you're on Facebook, send a message out to all your friends. Just don't forget you'll need to have an idea of the day and time your running group will meet before you start inviting people to join. One of the hardest things to do will be to get everyone together at the same time.

Once you've set up your club, you'll have to be consistent. A running club or group will get larger if you keep doing it regularly as the word will continually spread.

17. HAVE A GOAL OR TARGET TO RUN TO

It's always a good idea to think about and plan your route before you actually set off running. This way you'll know how far you've got to go, roughly how long it will take you and if there are any hills or difficult sections along the way. This way you can plan any rest points and be sure you know how to get back to base again.

18. WALK-JOG-WALK, DON'T RUN!

One of the very best ways of starting to run is by gently introducing small amounts of running each time you go out. An all-out effort, followed by nothing, is not a recipe for success. Instead try the walk, jog, walk approach. This way you walk for 30 seconds, jog for 30 seconds and then walk for 30 seconds etc. You keep repeating this pattern for the entire route. Of course, 30 seconds might not be right for you to begin with, you may need to do more or less - depending on your fitness level . But the point is this, break it down into small manageable chunks. Once you can easily complete your route this way then you can either decrease the amount of walking you do or run faster during the jogging parts.

19. GET OUTSIDE

There are a few drawbacks to running outside such as traffic, uneven footing, the risk of running into any undesirables etc. But apart from the fact that running outdoors is free and more stimulating there is an ever-changing panorama around every corner. Running outside also helps you to clear the airways and breathe in fresh air, as well as soak up Vitamin D from the sun (OK, maybe not if it's at night, but you get the point!)

If the other alternative is exercising in a sweat filled, air-conditioned fitness centre, pounding along on one of a row of treadmills, then you really need to rethink your strategy.

Recently, experts at the Peninsula College of Medicine and Dentistry concluded that exercising in a natural environment was shown to reduce tension, stress and feelings of anger and depression, whilst increasing energy levels and vitality.

So running outside isn't just more interesting, it's also better for your health!

20. KEEP CHANGING WHAT YOU DO

One of the biggest mistakes many people make in running and almost every area of fitness is to keep doing the same thing over and over again. Once your body has got used to working at a particular level, it takes it easy. It conserves calories and reduces heart and lung work. Don't forget that we're designed to be as efficient as possible. Unfortunately, this means that what you did at one time won't give you the same benefits all the time. So you'll need to chop and change things regularly to keep improving and getting fitter.

Ideally, you'll make some kind of change to what you're doing every workout - running faster, further, taking less rest, running up more hills and more often. These are just a few ways to keep improving your body.

21. KEEP YOUR RUNS SHORT AT FIRST AND BUILD UP GRADUALLY

Many beginners over face themselves with too difficult a task at first, making their initial runs too long and arduous. Remember Neil Armstrong's first words when landing on the moon... *'One small step for man, one giant step for mankind.'* This is true for something as simple as running. You won't get far enough to accomplish anything until you've taken those first few steps. These should be baby steps when you're just starting out, not daunting giant steps. Don't worry, you'll be able to build up your distances and speeds slowly and surely after this.

Another very important point to consider is that once you set a precedent in terms of how far and fast you run, doing anything less in the future will feel like a failure.

Lastly if you've taken your run to the point of pain or serious discomfort, the chances are that you won't feel like doing it again. As a result, you'll find it harder to motivate yourself to get out and run in the future.

You need to coax and encourage your body into change, not force it at gunpoint!

22. PLAN A FEW ROUTES

Don't get bogged down doing just one route, as you'll quickly get bored and reach a stagnation point with it. Instead devise a few routes that you can do based on the way you feel that particular day. For example, you should have some 10, 15, 20 and 30 minute routes that you can use, graded into easy, moderate and difficult runs. Also select some flat, scenic routes and some hilly or undulating runs.

Variety is the key and if you don't feel up to really going for a run one day or you're pushed for time, you can simply do one of your shorter or easier routes instead.

There are many great apps you can get for free that will help you to plot out how far and where you want to run to.

23. FOLLOW A TRAINING PLAN FOR BEGINNERS

There's a reason why most people who can afford to do so use trainers, coaches and mentors for sport. You can use their knowledge and experience to sidestep the usual learning curve that comes with any new sport or discipline.

If you can't afford to use a coach, then get hold of the best training plan you can. Make sure it's from a respected expert and follow it as closely as you can. If it's well written it should include a graduated training plan that gives you adequate rest and a range of running techniques you can use, to keep you progressing at the fastest rate possible whilst minimising the risk of injury.

24. USE INTERVAL TRAINING TO BOOST YOUR FITNESS LEVELS

Interval training is basically breaking a workout down into short bursts of higher intensity effort interspersed with lower intensity recovery phases. You can do this in many ways. The easiest for a beginner is to use segments of time for walking and running. You can control what these are, but need stick to them once you know what you're doing.

If you simply stop whenever you feel tired (working this way is more like Fartlek training), you won't make the same progress as you can do when you push past your comfort zone a little.

Interval training doesn't have to be cast in stone and you can also play around with distances. For example, you might be walking and see a sign in the distance, this would be a good point to run to - but don't stop until you get there!

25. VARY YOUR WORKOUTS

As you will vary the distances and speeds you run, you should also add in some different training techniques such as hills, pyramid training, intervals, Fartlek training and sprint sessions. The beauty of doing this is that it adds variety to your plan and helps increase your lactic acid threshold (the point at which your legs refuse to move any more!). It also improves the strength and endurance of your heart and lungs.

Having a range of different types of workout to do also means that if time is short one day, but you want to keep your training moving forwards, you can get an equally beneficial workout from doing a sprint or hill session instead. It's shorter to do, but you'll still be improving your fitness.

26. THINK ABOUT WHAT YOU WANT TO ACHIEVE

Firstly, you'll need to write out some running goals. This obviously depends on the reason why you're starting running... to run a 5km, a half marathon or even a full one.

Next, you'll need to plan out how you're going to get there. This includes writing down the days and times of the runs you intend to do. Plan around any potential problems, such as late work nights, or kid's clubs etc. Write out your plan at the beginning of every week so you know what you have to expect from yourself.

Finally have a think about the thing that always stops you from reaching your goals and create a plan of action to stop it happening again.

You may wonder why these things are so important, here's why...

- Without an end goal or a direction to head in we'll never reach our destination.
- Without actually doing our running, we'll never get any better.
- Without changing habits and attitudes, you'll simply get what you've always have done. Fine if you are always successful, but think carefully if this doesn't apply to you.

27. AIM FOR QUALITY NOT QUANTITY

Gone are the days when the only advice to get better at running was to run as far as you can for as long as you can. This is not an efficient use of your time. Following this strategy means that you won't make progress as quickly as you can, but also you're at a greater risk of injury due to the amount of running you'd need to do in order to improve.

Yes, you should do some steady state training (running at a constant speed or level of intensity), but it only needs to make up a part of your whole running regime.

Instead, try using advanced training techniques such as intervals, pyramids, hill reps, Fartlek or tempo training to vary your workouts and raise your running levels to a new level.

28. USE A TREADMILL IF IT'S COLD AND WET OUTSIDE

Many hardened runners don't like running on a treadmill They complain of the lack of fresh air, nothing to look at, being cooped up inside, a change in the technique needed to use it properly and the difficulty in getting access to one. Of course, one of the great things about running is you can start your workout as soon as you put your foot out of the front door.

However, depending on where in the world you live, there may very well be certain times in the year, when running outdoors becomes not only too dangerous, but virtually impossible. Treadmill running does require a slightly different running technique to hitting the roads, but at times when running outside means you risk injury or not being able to run at all, a treadmill is a very good replacement, just don't rely on it entirely.

29. RUN FOR CHARITY

Booking a place in a race and signing up to run in aid of a charity is a fantastic way to raise the profile of what you're doing and to increase your motivation to do the training in the first place. You'll be pushing yourself because of a feeling of responsibility to the charity, but you'll also be raising money for a worthy cause too. It's definitely a win – win situation!

30. NEVER RUN ON AN EMPTY STOMACH

If your goal is to become a better runner, you need to ensure that there's always fuel in the tank. If you're an early morning runner (well done, I salute you!) then you need to eat a small carbohydrate snack around an hour before you set off, this could be something as simple as a banana, an energy drink, a slice of toast with some fruit spread or a couple of oat cakes with peanut butter... just ensure you eat something.

Remember running first thing means that you're going out on an empty tank, you've effectively been fasting for many hours, so without any easy-to-use glycogen coursing through your blood stream, you may not be capable of running your best.

31. FOCUS ON YOUR BREATHING

One of the most common questions that newbie runners ask is how to breathe. The answer is quite simple, the purpose of breathing is to get as much oxygen into the blood stream to pass on to the muscles as quickly as possible. As we exercise the demand from our muscles for oxygenated blood rises which is why our breathing rate increases when we work harder.

The key here is to breathe in as slowly and deeply as possible to get as much air into our lungs as we can. The most efficient way to do this is to breathe in using both the nose and mouth at the same time. You need to make a conscious effort to slow down your breathing rate otherwise you'll end up panting and won't be able to inhale as much air as you need. When this happens, you'll quickly need to slow down or stop running altogether, until your breathing rate returns to normal and the amount of oxygen you breathe in can keep up with the demand for it from your muscles.

32. RELAX AND LET GO OF THE TENSION

Every time you run and push yourself a little harder, you'll be getting out of your comfort zone; your breathing rate will increase, you'll start to feel the lactic acid build up in the muscles and you'll feel the tension in your chest from your heart beating faster.

These are all things that could make you start to feel tense. What you need to do in order to get the most out of your run is to relax and try to slow down your breathing rate. Make a conscious effort to breathe in deeply and breathe out slowly. Focussing on the rate and depth of your breathing can often help you to get more out of your training runs before having to stop.

33. TRY CADENCE BREATHING

Cadence breathing is a great way to help you to get into the zone and to relax into your running. It also helps you to take your mind off any discomfort you may be experiencing and thoughts about other things that are going on in your life.

The way you cadence run is by breathing in over 3 or 4 steps and then breathing out over 3 or 4 steps. You can play around with the ratio anyway you like until you've found a speed and rate of breathing that suits you. You should feel in control, relaxed and calm. You can always return back to this breathing rate if you ever get breathless or are tackling some hills, sprints or intervals etc.

34. KEEP AN EYE ON YOUR FORM

Just as poor technique in the gym can lead to pulled muscles and joint injuries, so can a bad running technique. The very nature of running means that it's a repetitive sport - you perform exactly the same movements, hundreds and thousands of times throughout the course of your training. If your technique is bad and you're running with an accentuated inward knee movement - for example- it won't be long before the rest of your body starts to adjust to help compensate.

The most common times for your form to deteriorate are if you're nursing an injury or towards the end of your run as you begin to tire. To offset this, concentrate more on your posture and running technique as you get tired. Try to avoid letting everything go in an attempt to get through the latter stages. Instead hold yourself upright and as tall as you can.

35. RUNNING POSTURE

Here's a quick posture check that you can do on yourself the next time you go running to make sure that you're not putting your body at risk...

- Aim to 'run tall' with your head held high.
- Keep your shoulders down and back, with your chest out and tummy muscles pulled in tight and held in this position.
- You should run with a mid-foot to toe or heel to toe action. Your mid -foot or heel contacts the ground first and then rolls forwards onto your toes before pushing off again.
- Your feet should be pointing slightly out to the sides.
- Use your arms to power you along, but try to relax your shoulders and keep them level.

36. COMPLEMENT YOUR RUNNING WITH YOGA

Unfortunately, one of the downsides to running regularly is the effect it can have on your muscles, which may feel tight, sore and uncomfortable following a tough training run. There's no way around this I'm afraid. Whenever you push yourself out of your comfort zone or even following a steady session, there will be a certain amount of muscle tightness that needs stretching and loosening off.

One of the best ways of doing this is by stretching them out thoroughly by doing Yoga a couple of times a week. Ideally, you'll join a yoga class because this will give you a firm appointment each week, so you're less likely to skip your sessions.

It isn't sexy or glamorous, but this could very well be one of THE most beneficial additions to your running regime there is.

37. SHED A FEW POUNDS TO HELP YOU RUN FURTHER

It stands to reason that if you weigh less, there's not as much of you to carry around and so the effort it takes your heart, lungs and legs to propel you over the tarmac will also be far less. Running up hills, sprinting and off-roading will all feel more comfortable and less challenging. There will also be a substantial reduction in the stress that all of your joints, ligaments and tendons are put under.

Another important point about losing weight is that your posture will improve the lighter you are. Consequently, your running style may also feel easier and more natural.

38. BUILD MUSCLE TO RUN FASTER

Did you know that having just one just extra pound of muscle tissue can help you to burn through an average of around 35 – 50 extra calories a day. This means that any time spent training in the gym using weights, machines or your own body weight etc., can help you to lose any extra body fat you're storing and, as a result, help you run further, faster or for longer.

The key as with all exercise is consistency. Don't just do sporadic weight sessions because you won't see any noticeable results this way. Instead, get yourself a training program and then stick to it. You'll need to weight train at least a couple of times a week to see any real benefit, but the effort it takes is well worth the rewards you'll gain.

39. HOW TO STOP SHIN SPLINTS

Shin splints is a generic term given to pain felt in the lower leg around the front of the shin area. The cause of this can be varied, but more commonly is caused by a tightening or compression of the nerves, muscles or blood vessels down the front of the lower leg or a hairline fracture of the bone.

The usual reasons for shin splints are over-use or a sudden change in activity levels- placing excess stress on the muscles of the shins (*Tibialis anterior*). These muscles are not the largest or strongest in the body and can quickly become overloaded and fatigued.

To resolve this problem, you need to reduce your mileage, speed or volume of training considerably until the pain subsides. Once it has, you can start to build up again. You should also stretch the shin muscles every day and strengthen them every other day to build up stamina and flexibility in the area.

If you suffer any ill effects down the shins after a run, apply an ice pack (a sealed bag with frozen peas or sweetcorn is perfect for this) to the area for 15 – 20 minutes, to reduce swelling.

40. DON'T BE AN OBSESSIVE RUNNING BORE

Discovering running can feel like the dawning of a new age. Once you get the bug, it's something that you can't believe you've not tried earlier in life. The energy it gives you and the way it makes you feel and look leads many runners to sing its praises loudly to all and sundry. Unfortunately, not everyone will share your love of running. By all means give friends and family a brief synopsis of what you're up to, just don't bore them to death about it. You'll probably not get the positive reaction you were hoping for anyway.

If you really want to share your successes and failings with other like-minded people, the best bet is to join a running club and socialise or sign up for a few running forums. You'll be surprised at what you'll learn and you could make some really good friends in the process plus they'll be truly interested in what you have to say!

41. ALWAYS HAVE A PLAN B

Having a well-planned routine can usually keep you going, but things don't always go according to plan. Let's say that you want to challenge yourself to run a specific number of miles every day. You have the outdoors, so that should be easy for you, right? Well, not always.

Let's say that you plan your runs after you finish work, but a thunderstorm comes between you and your running routine. Unless you're a fan of running in torrential rain, your plan is ruined. Not to mention the fact that it will negatively impact your performance.

This is why you should always have a plan B. Perhaps you can get access to a gym or do some strength training at home instead. What's important is that you don't put the brakes on your daily activity completely. Once you do, it will be harder to get back on track.

42. USE APPS TO KEEP YOU RUNNING

If there's something that you can always rely on these days, it's technology. There's an app for everything – and you can be sure that there are hundreds of running apps. If you find a fitting app for you, it can pull you through even the hardest of runs, motivating you along the way.

These types of apps are perfect if you're a beginner. Some will track your progress. Others will give you motivational quotes whenever you reach a milestone. Some will even simulate your game as if you are in a zombie apocalypse. Depending on the app, it can do wonders to keep you entertained as you run.

43. REST AT CROSSWALKS

Many runners jog in place at pedestrian crossings (crosswalks) so that they maintain their steady breathing rate and body heat -preventing both from dropping. Many new runners do this, as they're afraid they'll lose their momentum if they stop running.

Still, when you are at a pedestrian crossing, you may want to use the opportunity to rest. It can help bring your breathing back under control, and it also allows you to check your posture. When the lights change and you can go, you can continue with your run.

Plus, it's safer for you to just stop instead of running in these places. If you are on the move, you may be tempted to start running once the light goes green. You will never know which driver will just try to power through, thinking they can save an extra few seconds. Since you are already running, they might not even notice you, which can put you in considerable danger.

2 CHAPTER DISTANCE RUNNING TIPS

1. STICK TO YOUR USUAL FOOD

The night before - or even worse- the morning before a long run is definitely not the time to be experimenting with a new food or drink. This also includes energy bars, drinks or protein shakes or anything that might improve your performance. You can't be sure how you'll react to anything new when you haven't tried it before and a long run is not the time to try it out. Stomach cramps, indigestion, diarrhoea or nausea are not things you want to experience when doing a 10 miler.

2. GET ORGANISED IN ADVANCE

Make you sure you know where you're going, have a good high carb meal a couple of hours before you set off and some water and you're good to go. A mobile phone, some money for bus or taxi fare (in case of any problems) and some form of identity are always good things to take with you in case the worst should happen.

3. WEAR THE RIGHT CLOTHING

Check the weather before you set off. If it's cold, get wrapped up by wearing a few light layers that you can remove when you start to warm up. If you're expecting rain, take a rain jacket and if it's windy, a hat. If you're running off-road you'll need to change your running shoes to cross trainers with more support and grip if you have any.

4. BREAK IT INTO CHUNKS

No matter how fit you are, it always helps to break distances down into smaller, more manageable chunks, if not for the body, then mainly for the mind. It's like any big task you undertake, but more so than most, because of the pain and discomfort you know you'll need to get through to achieve your goal of running the distance. Take it ten minutes or one mile at a time, just don't focus on the big picture when you're preparing for or just getting started on any longer runs.

5. PLAN YOUR JOURNEY

Sounds like an obvious thing to say I know, but if you're going to be clocking up the miles, you first need to know how far you'll be running and also plan to finish at the same place you start, so you don't have to worry about getting back home or to the car afterwards. Use an app to plot your route, or go 'old school' and get out in the car. Make a note of the milometer reading when you start and again when you finish- at least this way you'll know what to expect when you run it.

6. TAKE AN ENERGY DRINK WITH YOU

You will need a little more than a simple energy drink, which tend to be full of sugars. In fact you'll need a drink that can help to replace lost electrolytes, which can become depleted through excessive sweating and exhaling over longer periods of time.

Here's a great isotonic energy drink that you can make yourself. It contains simple sugars and sodium to keep you running your best.

- 250ml/ 9fl oz pure unsweetened fruit juice
- 750ml/ 25fl oz warm water
- 1.5g sea salt

7. DON'T EAT A CURRY THE NIGHT BEFORE A LONG ONE!

If you do need to eat out the night before a run , don't go for anything too spicy as this can easily upset your tummy the morning after - definitely not a good a pre-race food. Ideally you'll eat a high carbohydrate meal with a little protein and containing good fats, such as Spaghetti Bolognaise or rice with a Chicken Stir Fry.

8. NEVER RUN THROUGH AN INJURY

Injuries can seriously hinder your performance at the best of times. A slight niggle can alter your stride pattern and place increased stress on other muscle groups and joints. Running any longer distances when you're carrying an injury can lead to serious long term damage. It's never what we want to hear, but when we get injured, we need to back off and get the injury looked at by a qualified therapist.

Sometimes you've got to rest and back off a little in order to make any future progress.

9. REST YOUR LEGS

After any long runs of above 60 minutes or so, rest your legs after running by keeping them elevated for 30 minutes. This helps to redistribute blood flow to the rest of the body instead of diverting more of it to the lower half of your body. Stretching off and rubbing some massage oil over the muscles for a few minutes will also help.

A little later the same day, going for a gentle walk is also a good idea as this helps to increase the blood flow back to muscles in the legs, which then helps to send protein- rich blood to help repair and renew damaged muscle tissue.

10. IMPROVE YOUR STAMINA BY CROSS TRAINING

If your goal is to run a half or full marathon, you'll need to build stamina and strength in the muscles of the legs and to strengthen the heart and lungs. The standard strategy is to do one longer run every week to gradually increase the distances you can keep going for. This isn't the only way you can do this.

Cross training using other types of exercise which build stamina in the muscles and the cardiovascular system are also very good choices because they remove the stresses and strains from the same muscles and joints as used in running. Activities including swimming, cycling and rowing are all great additions to your regime and should be done once a week to add much-needed variety.

11. UNLOAD A BIT OF BAGGAGE BEFORE YOU SET OFF

If you always need to stop during your longer runs for a 'number 1' (a wee!) then here's a strategy that might help a little. It's important that your body is fully hydrated. Don't go out without making sure you've had a drink or two. It's the timing of these drinks that's critical.

To maximise your hydration levels without the risk of having to stop on your long runs, drink approximately 500ml - 2 hours before you run. (it takes an average of 60 minutes for your body to digest and absorb 500ml of water). Then go to the toilet just before you run. Throughout your run you'll need to sip very small amounts of water as you go along. This water will be needed to replace lost sweat as you go, so you should be fine.

12. HARNESS THE POWER OF THE MIND

Even if your training is going perfectly, there will always come a point when you're struggling to make any further progress and you hit a wall (no, not literally!). When this time comes, you have two options, you either stop where you are and go back, or you find a way around the wall. I obviously prefer the second option, as without this approach, you'll get nowhere in life.

So here's a little mind programming technique you can use on your next run.

We all have a certain sticking point, be that getting to the top of a particular hill, being able to keep going for longer than 5 miles, running at a specific tempo for a set amount of time etc.

Whatever your sticking point is, I want to you to start visualising getting past it. I want you to imagine how it feels, what things look like, the sounds you'll hear and what you can smell. I want you to visualise the experience as clearly as if you were actually doing it, as in your mind, you're going to beat the challenge. Not just once, but every time you think about it from now on. Don't make your task unattainable. It should be only just out of reach at the moment, but you're going to start believing you can do it.

To do this effectively, you need to be fully relaxed, in a quiet, warm and comfortable room, with a little relaxing music gently playing in the background and ideally in a lying or reclined position. Try to slow down your breathing and fully relax your muscles before playing the scene through in minute detail in your mind. Don't have any doubts that you can do it. In your mind you can and in your body you will too!

13. ARE YOU DOING TOO MUCH?

Whilst it's wonderful to have a hobby or an interest that you're passionate about, there will always be a point in any type of exercise at which you're doing too much and this is known as over-training. Running is no different. You'll be challenging your whole body every time you run; not only in terms of your heart and lungs, but also the stresses and strains you are placing on your nervous system - which can easily become overloaded.

Everyone is different. What is excessive to some, will be fine for others, but if or when this time arrives, you'll show certain signs and symptoms. These can be wide and varied but the most common ones are:

- Fatigue
- Nausea
- Lack of interest in exercise
- Trouble sleeping at night

- Loss of appetite
- Constant soreness or excessive aching in the muscles

Over-training is common and you'll have to learn when it's your body telling you to take it easy or your head trying to convince you it's time for a rest. If you're doing too much, you'll also be more susceptible to any colds, bugs or viruses going around.

14. BANISH BLISTERS

Blisters can be the bane of many runners' lives, halting progress in an instant and turning what could have been a very productive training run or race into a painful experience you just want to get over and done with as quickly as possible. If you've tried sticking plasters, specialist running socks or different shoes and the problem still persists, try applying petroleum jelly to the troublesome areas to reduce friction or wearing two pairs of thin socks which rub against each other instead of your feet as this can sometimes work. Here's a link to a good running sock retailer – *www.runbreeze.com*

If neither of these techniques work for you, then I recommend that you try this alternative strategy to alleviate the blight.

When you finish your next run and you've got a blister/ blisters, soak your feet in hot, salty water for 20 – 30 minutes. The effect of the salty water is to draw moisture out and away from the blisters. Once soaked, remove your feet from the water and allow them to dry thoroughly in the open air. Repeat this technique for the next few weeks after each run and see how the problem is improved.

15. EAT EVERY HOUR

When you're running for longer periods of time - at least 90 minutes- you'll need to eat or drink some form of sugar to replace lost glycogen stores.

On average the muscles and liver can store up to 2,000 calories in the form of glycogen- which is enough to run 18 miles. However it's best not to wait until energy stores are depleted before eating. Instead, keep them topped up by munching on a handful of jelly beans, an energy gel or an isotonic sports drink (hypotonic drinks are designed to rehydrate, whereas isotonic are best for refuelling) every 60 minutes. Test this out first though, don't try using it in a race until you're happy with the results.

16. MIX UP YOUR RUNNING ROUTINE

Going through the same routine every day can seem pretty boring. One week into a 30-day running challenge, you may already be bored out of your mind with seeing the same scenery. You might even decide not to go *"just for today,"* simply because you don't feel like it.

When this happens, you may want to change your routine a little. Take the bus to another loop that you haven't run before, or maybe join a local running marathon. Running to a specific destination may also spice things up. Going on runs should be a fun activity. When things start feeling stale, mix things up a bit.

17. TRY LISTENING TO AN AUDIOBOOK WHILE RUNNING

When you are running long distances, things can get very boring on the road. Listening to music on the run can help take the edge off, but it risks taking away all of your senses. If the music is too loud, not only will you not be able to hear traffic and people around you, it can also distract you from your pace.

Indeed, some songs can keep you running better, but you can also try an audio-book. It doesn't have any strong bass or loud songs, so a decent volume will still let you hear the things around you. It will keep you safe while running, and also keep your mind preoccupied while you do it.

Plus, when you're listening to the plot in an audio-book, you will be so absorbed that you won't notice how the time is passing. If you are running a marathon, where distance is more important than speed, it will help you power through as you will be captivated by the story.

18. PLAN YOUR ROUTE AROUND BATHROOMS

Nothing feels worse than having to run with a full bladder and having nowhere to stop to relieve the problem. Many runners stop midway through a run and turn around, caving into their desire to use the toilet. Those who try to power through will also risk losing their pace, because running will only make the matter feel worse.

A good idea is to plan a route that has at least one or two bathrooms along the way. You'll still have to wait before you reach them, but at least it won't cause you to abandon your run. Plus, the short bathroom breaks can be beneficial, as these resting minutes can help bring your breathing pattern back under control.

19. RUN FOR TIME INSTEAD OF DISTANCE

Finding the time to run can be very challenging sometimes, especially if you have a full-time job ahead of you. Running for distance means spending a lot of time running and it often messes up your schedule. You may have a certain amount of time on your hands, so running for a distance can cause you to stop before you reach your mileage goal.

This is why you should run for time instead of distance. Not only will it help you stay organised, it can also improve your motivation. If you reach your running time goal every session, you'll be less likely to quit halfway through your challenge.

Plus, the more you run, the faster you get. When your speed improves, you'll be able to run more miles in the same amount of time - so you'll get a better workout. This is more appropriate for your fitness level than just running a chosen distance.

20. RUN MORE HILLS

There is a saying that hill running is strength training in disguise. For sprinters and distance runners, this can give an exercise boost. After all, you are mixing speed with a kind of resistance training in one exercise and yes, dragging your weight up a hill does double as weight training.

Running up hills can improve your cardiovascular fitness while improving your running form and reducing the impact on your joints. Since you're using more effort to run up hills, your endurance will also improve. You will see that once you start running on the flat again, you will be able to run much further.

3
CHAPTER

SAFETY **TIPS**

1. IF YOU RUN OFF ROAD GET THE CORRECT GEAR

Treadmill and road running are perfect for traditional running shoes which have a lot of cushioning and minimal grip, but if you plan on going off-road quite a bit, then you'll need to get yourself some shoes specifically for this. These shoes need to be more supportive around the ankles. Suitable shoes tend to be heavier with less cushioning and bigger grips on the sole.

2. NEW RUN - LEAVE THE HEADPHONES AT HOME

If you're running along busy streets or you don't know an area, it's vital that you're fully aware of your surroundings. By wearing headphones to listen to music, you're taking away one of your most important senses (sound) which could be a big mistake. You won't hear traffic, other pedestrians, potential hazards etc.

Another factor is that when you listen to music, you tend to go into your own world and get absorbed by the melodies - not really taking in your surroundings. You'll also miss out on crucial noises that may help you to find your way back to your starting point if you end up getting lost. These sounds may not be loud or specific, but they help our subconscious minds to make sense of our surroundings at all times.

3. DON'T TURN UP THE VOLUME TOO LOUD

Everybody likes a bit of extra motivation when they run – especially as they start to tire. However, turning the music up the max, isn't always the best thing to do. If you're running around busy streets, then you're probably safe from the local hoodlums, but you won't hear the juggernaut steaming past your shoulder and making a hard left turn in front of you. If you're running down quiet country lanes, you might not hear any other possible threats.

So by all means listen to your favourite music, but don't crank it up too high, otherwise you effectively lose one of your five essential senses.

4. TAKE YOUR MOBILE WITH YOU

One of the reasons why you've taken up running might be to take a break from life. You may well want to get away from everyone for a while to enjoy some well-earned 'Me' time and you might not want to be contacted when you're out. You can turn your mobile phone off, but take it with you anyway. It's important that you have a means of getting in touch with someone in case of emergency.

You never know when you might get lost, run too far, develop an injury, get tired or run into any kind of difficulty that means you need a lift home. Any of these factors could place you in a very difficult situation. At least if you carry your phone with you, you can switch it on and contact someone if needed.

5. ALWAYS RUN FACING ONCOMING TRAFFIC

When you run always face oncoming traffic so you can see what's coming towards you and if necessary, take evasive action to avoid it. Even wearing high visibility clothing doesn't always mean that you'll be seen by other road users. Motorists may be dazzled by other car headlights, they may have ice on their windscreen or fog on the inside of the glass. Any of these factors may mean they don't see you running towards them until it's too late.

Facing traffic allows YOU to be more in control and more aware of your surroundings.

4 CHAPTER NUTRITIONAL TIPS **FOR RUNNERS**

1. EAT STRAIGHT AFTER YOUR RUN

Experts agree that the perfect time to eat in order to help speed up the recovery process after running is within 60 minutes of finishing the run. There's a small window of opportunity in which your body soaks up nutrients like a sponge. During this time, you're far less likely to store any extra calories as body fat because you need to replenish the glycogen stores which have been depleted during the run. Your muscles and connective tissues need proteins to help them to repair and renew their damaged cells.

Soon after running, try to eat a good balanced meal of lean proteins, starchy carbohydrates (potatoes, rice, pasta etc.) and fibrous carbs (broccoli, spinach, cauliflower etc.) along with some mono and polyunsaturated fats (olive, rapeseed, ground nut oil etc.). If you want to have a bit of a splurge or more of a treat food, now might be the best time to do it!

2. EAT A GOOD BREAKFAST

Perhaps the most important meal of the day is breakfast. Studies show that people who eat breakfast are far less likely to suffer energy lows mid-morning, are sharper and more focussed and less prone to be overweight.

From a weight management point of view, it makes logical sense to eat your largest meal at the beginning of the day, when you have many hours of movement ahead of you, rather than eating it last thing at night just before bed.

For runners this is even more important because it's the first opportunity in the day to top up depleted glycogen stores following the fasting time during sleep. If you set off for any run with low levels of fuel in the tank, it won't be long before you start to struggle.

A good balanced breakfast for runners could include a glass of fruit juice, some wholemeal toast with jam and a bowl of no added sugar muesli. However, if you're also trying to manage your weight, this could be a little excessive unless you make allowances both in terms of the amount of exercise you do and the foods you eat during the rest of the day.

3. DON'T OVEREAT

It is important to eat a wide range of healthy foods to ensure glycogen stores are kept topped up as a runner, but there is certainly no need to overeat. As with all things, moderation is the key.

Running burns calories, raises the metabolic rate and you may very well find an increase in your appetite. The further you run, the more calories you'll burn and the hungrier you'll feel. However, even if the foods you choose are from healthy sources, if you overeat and consume more than you burn off, you will gain weight.

Any increase in body fat stores is not going to help you get fitter, however, you may well gain muscle weight, meaning you'll be heavier, but more powerful and also more efficient at burning through calories. So, keep an eye on the weighing scales and periodically monitor what's happening with your weight. Don't simply assume that because you're running regularly, you are losing weight.

4. GET ORGANIZED

There's one reason why even the most motivated and dedicated runners turn to ready meals or unhealthy snacks between meals, and that's a lack of organisation or time. The secret to success in getting the best out of your nutrition is to be organised and prepared for when you need food the most.

If there's one thing that will seal your fate in terms of not eating a balanced diet, it's simply not having the right foods available to you when you're hungry.

The solution is easy... have all of the foods you need, ready and waiting for you whenever you need them. Ideally washed, chopped and prepared in 'ready to go' tubs, bags or packets. This way it's far easier to to eat these wholesome foods as opposed to turning to the convenience and speed of junk food.

5. DON'T FORGET TO DRINK

Make it your goal to drink at least 2 litres of water every day, because nothing can impact your running performance more than your body becoming dehydrated.

Water is vitally important to the body, without it we can't perform at our best. However it's not always easy to work out if you're dehydrated or not as thirst cannot be used as an accurate indicator to your fluid status. When you feel thirsty, you're probably already dehydrated. Don't wait until you feel you need a drink, but instead sip small amounts, regularly throughout the day.

Water, milk and sugar-free drinks can all be counted towards this 2 litre daily target, but fruit juices and sugary drinks are termed as HYPERTONIC. This means they contain a higher concentration of sugar than found in the blood and therefore they can't be used in the same way to help maintain or top up normal fluid levels.

TOP TIP - Try keeping a 2 litre bottle of water in the refrigerator and pour your drinks from this throughout the day to ensure you're drinking the correct amount.

6. EAT TO RUN

Before a run, select foods that are easy to digest and give a good energy boost. Try to stay away from high fat foods or dense proteins such as red meats. These take quite a while for your body to break down and require plenty of time to be digested fully.

A small snack might take around 30 – 60 minutes to metabolise, whereas a larger meal could take a minimum of 2 – 3 hours - depending on what foods you've eaten. Generally speaking, simple carbs such as white bread, pasta or sugars will be absorbed into the blood stream more quickly, but are usually followed by an energy sapping low soon after.

So for longer runs, try filling up on whole grain products for a slower, steadier release of energy.

7. SNACKING CAN BOOST YOUR PERFORMANCE

Relying on the old staple of 'three meals a day' is an outdated concept for those of us who are active- especially if we're aiming to become better runners. Not only does regular snacking boost your metabolic rate, but for those who participate in regular sports, it also provides a constant and ready supply of energy.

When we have blood sugar lows such as those experienced when there are large gaps between meals, our body begins to crave high fat, high sugar foods, in order to give us a much-needed calorie boost. Instead of munching on junk food and making matters worse, why not try snacking on raw unsalted nuts, fresh fruit or reduced fat hummus with carrot, celery or cucumber sticks?

8. TREAT YOURSELF TO A CHOCOLATE MILK

Many top runners swear by the virtues of drinking chocolate milk straight after running and studies have proven its positive effects. This idea has a number of benefits. Firstly drinking chocolate milk straight after exercising will have very little impact on the amount of calories stored as fat, in fact quite the opposite. The nutrients in the chocolate milk consumed at this time are far more likely to be sent to the muscles to replace used fuel or to aid in the repair of damaged muscle and connective tissue cells.

Last but not least - it tastes great, so it's a wonderful treat to look forward to after your session.

9. TAKE A DAILY MULTI–VITAMINS

As an active individual, you'll have to ensure that your nutrition supplies you with everything you need. Unfortunately however, because of modern farming techniques this means that some of the foods that we eat may not be as nutritionally dense as they once were. When you combine this with the processing, longer delivery journeys and shelf lives of some of our foods, it's no wonder that by the time we get to eat them, they don't quite deliver all the nutritional benefits we need.

Because of this, it's a very good idea to take a multi-vitamin supplement to allow for any deficiencies that naturally occur in your diet - even if you eat a wide range of healthy, nutritious foods. Running regularly is one of those times where any shortfall will be exposed and can potentially leave you vulnerable to bugs and viruses or not recovering quickly enough between sessions. For a few coins a day, the cost of a tub of good multi-vitamins is well worth it in the end.

10. DILUTE YOUR BREAKFAST OR PRE-RUN FRUIT JUICE

A good start to the day is to drink a glass of freshly squeezed fruit juice. However if you mix it 50/50 with water, you're still getting all the nutrients from the juice, but it slows down the absorption of the sugars into the bloodstream which means you'll avoid the usual blood sugar highs followed by the energy sapping lows.

It's also a great tip for saving money and making food go a little further.

11. HAVE SOMETHING SWEET BEFORE YOUR RUN

While you shouldn't make a full meal out of candy before your run, it is not a bad idea to have a small, sweet snack. This can offer you a much-needed sugar boost, which is much welcome for that last-minute motivation. So, don't be afraid to grab a handful of *Skittles* or *Haribo's* (or any other well-known brand of sugary snack!!) as you dash out the door. After all, you'll burn off those calories during your run anyway.

However, if you're running for weight loss, try eating some fruit instead. Some good options are mangoes, cherries, grapes, watermelons, pears, and bananas. The natural sugar dose you get from these fruits should be enough to keep you energised throughout your run.

12. ENJOY A CUP OF COFFEE BEFORE YOUR MORNING RUN

Now, we know that many runners have this routine: wake up, grab their gear, and get out the door without any coffee or breakfast. While efficient and as quick this may be, this may actually be slowing down your progress. Knowing that breakfast is far away, you could feel less motivated to get up and begin your run.

Having said that, if you enjoy a cup of coffee before your morning runs, you'll at least have something else to get out of bed for. As a coffee enthusiast, you're probably familiar with the boost of happiness you get when you drink your favourite cup of Joe. Waking up 15 minutes earlier is worth it - especially since you'll also get a welcome caffeine boost before your run.

13. REWARD YOURSELF WITH A GOOD BREAKFAST AFTER TRAINING

A good way to stay motivated for a run is to reward yourself with a delicious breakfast after you finish. Let's say that you set yourself a goal of running for 30 minutes, then after your run, you can get some delicious pancakes and a fancy cappuccino. Not only will this act as motivation, but it will also strengthen your willpower.

On the other hand, this may also prove beneficial for your body. When you run, you burn a fair number of calories. If you don't eat something within the first 30 minutes of your workout, this can cause you to feel fatigued, so you need to nourish your body.

By making it tasty too, not only do you give yourself nourishment, but you also have something to look forward to. You'll be more likely to run with enthusiasm when you know you'll enjoy a great breakfast afterwards.

5 CHAPTER RUNNING KIT **ADVICE**

1. WEAR CYCLING SHORTS OR SKINS UNDER YOUR RUNNING SHORTS

There are two reasons for this. Firstly if you're running when it's cold, wearing a thinner, tight-fitting pair improves insulation and helps to keep you warm.

Secondly, wearing a layer made of Lycra or Elastene next to your skin, reduces the amount of chafing or friction caused by other running short materials rubbing against your skin. Incidentally, the trade term for this material is *Spandex*, which is an anagram of the word 'expands'

2. BUY RUNNING GEAR THAT YOU LIKE THE LOOK OF

OK, it might only be gear that you're running in that will be getting sweaty, wet and sometimes muddy, but nevertheless, that doesn't mean that you can't look good in it. Running clothing has evolved massively over the last few decades. Not only has running clothing become more lightweight, breathable and practical, it is now available in a huge range of colours and styles for both men and women.

There's certainly no excuse for looking shoddy when running the streets these days.

3. SPARKLE AND SHINE

It's quite possible that you'd prefer to blend into the background when you go out running instead of standing out like a sore thumb, but unfortunately that's EXACTLY what you should be doing.

It's important that you can be seen, during the day and especially at night if you're running on roads. For this reason, you should either buy bright, light colours such as whites, yellows or oranges or invest in some luminous strips to attach to your clothing. The trend these days is for black with luminous patches and stripes already attached which is fine, just don't cover up these reflective parts with other items of clothing.

The reflective effects of the luminous panels on your clothes will catch in the headlights of passing motorists, pedestrians and other road users and keep you safe and seen at night.

4. CHERISH YOUR RUNNING SHOES

One of the most common ways of storing wet running shoes to maintain their shape and to help them dry out is to fill them full of newspaper. This is effective because the paper helps to absorb any moisture from sweat, mud or rainwater etc. and draws it out of the fabric, helping to maintain the shape and structure of the shoe.

However, I've always felt that doing this left them feeling a little loose when I came to wear them again, so I've always used tip #5 instead.

5. USE KITTY LITTER TO BANISH ODOURS

This could be one of the strangest running tips you will ever hear, just remember to use the stuff from a fresh bag, not from your cat's litter tray!!

This tip is courtesy of one of my running clients who uses the technique himself... and has a cat.

When your running shoes get wet, be that through sweat, water or mud etc., pour kitty litter into them to absorb the moisture and odours. Kitty litter contains a carbon type substance that helps to absorb moisture and neutralise bad smells (not that your running shoes would ever be smelly or sweaty of course!)

Simply fill up your shoes with kitty litter and leave for 24 hours to do its job. Carefully empty out your running shoes and quickly vac or brush clean them to have beautifully smelling, fresh and dry running shoes.

6. STOP THE BOUNCE

Over 50% of women runners complain of breast pain when running which could be alleviated through the use of wearing a suitable correctly fitting bra. As a female runner, one of the first things on your shopping list after running shoes has to be a good, well- fitting sports bra.

Ideally you'll get properly measured for this as without sufficient support, the ligaments that help to hold breast tissue in place can become stretched and looser. Once this has happened, there is more likelihood that your breasts will appear saggy and droopy.

Your bra needs to fit snugly and feel comfortable without pinching the skin or hindering your breathing. Manufacturers recommend replacing sports bras every 40 washes to maintain their quality (but they would wouldn't they!)

7. CHANGE YOUR RUNNING SHOES REGULARLY

Your running shoes get a lot of stick. They'll run through water, mud, ice, snow, on tarmac, over grass and on gravel during the course of their life span. You name it, your shoes have done it and the sad truth is that running shoes aren't meant to last forever. The support under the heels and mid-foot tends to wear out over time and become redundant -especially if you're a little overweight or naturally heavy-footed.

You should look to buying a new pair of running shoes once you've run around 350 - 400 miles in them. When they get to this point, they've probably outlived their usefulness to you and you need to bite the bullet and buy another pair.

8. WEAR YOUR NEW SHOES AS SLIPPERS

When you decide to buy a new pair of running shoes, don't throw them on and dash out for an excited 10 miler to see how they feel. Instead you'll need to 'break them in' properly at first. Use them in place of slippers around the house and garden for a couple of weeks, until they've adjusted to your foot shape and size.

This is an important point and one you ignore at your peril. You need to break the new shoes in gradually, perhaps by doing a few walks or shorter runs until they feel more natural to you.

Remember, your old shoes have had months (or even years in some cases) to mould to the shape of your feet and the style of running you have - your new ones need to be given time to do the same.

9. BUY YOUR RUNNING SHOES LATER IN THE DAY

As you move around throughout the course of the day, your feet expand and swell and so buying running shoes first thing in the morning may give you a slightly different fitting to if you try them on later in the day. As you run, your feet will also fill out more, so it's important that you have a good fitting shoe.

Wearing a pair of your normal running socks when you go to buy shoes is a very handy tip as this will give you a more accurate idea as to how well your new shoes fit.

10. TRY THE JOHN MCENROE LOOK

Sorry if you're under 35 or haven't watched any old tennis video footage, you probably won't have seen the legendary tennis player John McEnroe play. His signature look was a sweat band around his forehead which helped to keep both sweat and his long curly hair out of his eyes.

Now you may not have long curly hair that stops you from seeing where you're going, but if not, I'm sure there have been times when rain water or sweat does irritatingly work its way down your forehead and into your eyes.

If you don't fancy getting a sweat band to wear around your head and run the risk of looking like an out-of-touch middle-aged man, then you could consider wearing a baseball cap or a bandana instead. If you're a woman, a running headband is a very fashionable piece of kit these days (actually I've seen men wearing these too!). If you don't like the idea of any of these, then a really good tip is to apply a thin line of Vaseline in an inverted 'v' shape on your forehead to divert the drips of sweat away from the eyes.

11. DON'T CONSTANTLY CHECK YOUR RUNNING WATCH

Sports watches are a great thing to keep yourself aware of your progress and can be a great incentive when running. Still, just as they can give you a morale boost, they can also lead to your running downfall. Ideally, you should leave your running watch at home – but if you don't want to, make sure you don't constantly stare at it.

When you do this, you'll be constantly comparing your mileage and progress with your last run. If you are having a bad running week, this will make your morale sink and chisel away at your motivation. It can even cause you to run slower or quit halfway through- simply because you are disappointed with yourself.

Rather than checking throughout the run, you should mostly check your watch at the end of the activity. This will allow you to keep your morale high and maintain your sprint as usual. And remember: we all have bad days. A slower run during the day shouldn't make you think that you can't beat your PB again.

12. WEAR SUPPORTIVE/COMPRESSION CLOTHING

You often hear about how important it is to buy supportive shoes for your running and that is advice to heed. But what about the rest of your clothes? The chances are that when you go running, you do so in loose clothing to feel more comfortable. Many of us are guilty of this, as it prevents our skin from feeling "sticky" under our clothes.

Having said that, supportive or compression clothing can be more beneficial to your body while you run. It will apply extra heat and pressure on your muscles, reducing the vibrations and therefore reducing risk of injury. Not only will you feel less sore after the run, but it could also prevent you from tiring too quickly.

Supportive clothing makes it more comfortable for you to run. The last thing you want is to feel your body jiggling continuously as you're running. This will lead to a new type of pain and discomfort. By wearing supportive clothing, you make sure everything stays in place, which will lead to a more enjoyable (but just as effective) run.

13. INVEST IN A PAIR OF SHOCK ABSORBING INSOLES

You may have a good pair of running shoes, but as a runner, it is also good to invest in shock absorption insoles. This should especially be the case when you run on hard surfaces such as tarmac or concrete. For those who do most of their runs in the city and on pavements, this can help reduce fatigue and even the risk of blistering.

Bear in mind that a pair of insoles with too much cushioning may add extra weight to your shoes. Go for insoles with limited cushioning thickness to reduce this. Memory foam insoles can be quite helpful, as they provide cushioning while following the exact shape of your foot. The better the quality of the insoles, the more support you'll get, and the farther you will be able to run.

14. DON'T WEAR COTTON ON RAINY DAYS

While many runners avoid going out on their routine run on a rainy day, others embrace it. There may also be instances when the rain is unexpected, giving you a surprise soaking. Whether you knew about the rainy day or not, you have to gear up appropriately - so it's best that you avoid wearing cotton clothing at all costs.

Cotton absorbs water, which can feel very uncomfortable on your skin even if it stops raining. It will make you feel cold, and the fabric will stick to your skin. Polyester or merino wool are the better bets, as they have thermal properties and are more breathable. Even if it rains, you'll still feel much warmer and more comfortable.

Cotton gear can also lead to chafing when it becomes wet. This may cause significant discomfort as you run, causing you to call it quits well ahead of time. Good gear can wick the moisture away from your skin, allowing you to finish your run just as you planned to do. Plus, aside from keeping the rainwater away from your skin, the correct clothing can also absorb sweat, preventing you from smelling too much.

6 CHAPTER GENERAL RUNNING TIPS

1. INCREASE YOUR MILEAGE BY NO MORE THAN 5 – 10% A WEEK

What this basically means is to build up your distances slowly and gradually. Many runners do too much in an attempt to move forwards with their training. They start seeing results and feel that doing more will give them even more progress. Unfortunately, there is a fine line between doing enough and doing too much. Overstep the mark and you run the risk of all types of injuries. You should gently coax your body along and using the 5 - 10% rule will help you to make a definite progression into your training - instead of just guessing.

So if you ran 2 miles in week 1, then week 2 should be no more than 2.2 miles etc.

2. TRY NOT TO TAKE BIG LUNGING STEPS

It's great to feel that you're full of energy and enthusiasm, but taking huge bounding steps is not going to help you progress in the least. You're increasing the impact on your ankles, knees, hips and lower back and are not running very efficiently. This means your progress will be much slower than it should be and you'll struggle to increase your speeds and reduce your average minutes per mile.

Instead, you should use a mid foot/heel strike to toe push off and almost glide your feet low over the ground, keeping your centre of gravity as low as possible as you run. This way you'll be moving forwards with every step instead of up, down and then forwards.

3. DON'T RUN ON SURFACES THAT COMPROMISE YOUR STYLE

Obviously, that doesn't mean never to run on paths or run on surfaces that aren't flat, but you should make sure these only make up a small percentage of your total running route and not the majority of it.

If you spend too long running on a slope (one foot higher than the other) then you will be placing too much stress on your hips, ankles, knees and lower back muscles, as well as the ligaments around your knees and the illio tibial band. You'll find that other joints and muscles will make allowances for the position you're running in and will compensate in order to keep you running, it's these adjustments that put you at a greater risk of injury.

4. ICE ON - ICE OFF

If you pick up any injuries when you're running, your first action should be to ice it. Remember the Acronym – RICE.

Rest the injured area. You'll do this by stopping running and immobilising or taking the weight off the injured area.

Ice the affected area. A cool pack, ice cubes in a towel or frozen peas or sweetcorn are ideal for the job. Don't apply the ice for longer than 20 minutes at a time, but remove the ice and apply it again an hour later. The reason for this short duration is to prevent frostbite.

Cases have been reported of frost bite affecting the toes of the patients who went on to suffer long term damage, so don't keep the ice on for any longer than 15 – 20 minutes at a time. Also, a good idea is to wrap the ice in a cloth to prevent it making direct contact with the skin. (if it's a toe or finger, you should reduce the icing time to no more than 10 minutes)

The ice helps to reduce swelling and inflammation. Applying ice this way also relieves pain and diverts blood flow away from the injury. Once the ice is removed there will be a surge of nutrient rich blood to help nourish and repair the damaged cells.

The last 2 letters in the 'RICE' acronym stand for **C**ompression (keep something tightly wrapped over it) and **E**levation (raising the injured area to reduce blood flow to it)

5. REWARD YOURSELF WHEN YOU REACH NEW HIGHS

It's a wonderful feeling to achieve your personal best at any time of life, or any level of ability, but it's especially great when you're a beginner and you see the changes unfolding in front of your eyes. When you consider where you started from, getting better at running is a very measurable sport. You can actually record how much further; faster and easier your running is becoming.

At each of the milestones you reach, why not reward yourself with an appropriate treat... a new pair of running shoes, an MP3 player or a running watch? These are all great ideas.

Doing this also ties in really well with goal setting as you can set a target of maybe reaching a set distance, or running without rest for a given amount of time and then when you accomplish this, you can reward yourself a treat.

6. GET YOURSELF A GADGET TO BOOST MOTIVATION

A heart rate monitor, pedometer or GPS running watch are all great ways to keep running fresh and interesting. By charting as many elements as you can with your running, you'll be able to clearly monitor your progress as time goes on.

Not only will these things clearly show you how your fitness levels are increasing, they're also great for keeping a record of how many steps you walk or how many calories you're burning every day. These factors are very useful if you're using running to shed a few excess pounds.

7. USE YOUR NOSE IF ITS COLD

One of the biggest problems runners face when running in the cold is that of breathing. When you start to breathe heavily and begin gasping for breath, taking a big gulp of freezing cold air can actually send your lungs into spasm (coughing) as well as feeling a sharp, painful rasp of the air passing down through your windpipe.

The secret here is to breathe in through your nose. Doing this has two main benefits. Firstly, when you breathe in through your nose, the air has further to go before it reaches your lungs, so it warms up before reaching them. Secondly, the nose contains thousands of tiny hairs which help to filter and warm the air far more efficiently than taking it straight in through your mouth.

8. GIVE YOUR LUNGS A WORKOUT

If you struggle with your breathing when running and it seems to be the one thing really holding you back, why not try to strengthen and increase the strength and stamina of your lungs? It's very easy to do and fully supported and endorsed by many experts and coaches worldwide. All you need is a special handheld breathing device called a 'POWERbreathe.

Basically, you perform some simple breathing exercises into the 'POWERbreathe' over a given length of time or number of exercises and this builds up strength and stamina in the lungs that you can fully utilise on your runs. To find out more log onto – *www.powerbreathe.com*

9. MAKE RUNNING PART OF YOUR LIFE

Lack of time is a real problem for many people and to suddenly add another hobby or interest, may just stretch the demands on your waking hours a little too far. To solve this problem, why not turn running into an integral part of your life so you just do it as part of another activity or task instead of dedicating some specific time to it on its own?

For example, how about running home from work a couple of times each week?

Alternatively, if you often work away from home and spend much of your time in hotels, why not take your running kit and go out in the evenings instead?

If you travel to and from work using buses or trains, how about getting changed into your running gear at work and getting off a stop or two earlier and running the rest of the way? How about going for a run when you drop the kids off at school or whilst waiting to pick them up when they have finished their after school clubs? You could easily be doing something instead of sitting there waiting. Why not pick an evening or two each week and run to a friend or family member's house? This way you can combine socialising with running... a perfect blend.

10. STEAL AN HOUR OR TWO

Nearly everyone can find the time to do a little extra something if it matters enough to them. I'm sure that if I told you that I'd pay you a million dollars if you could find a spare one or two hours a week, you'd find them from somewhere!

But where can you get this time from? You can't invent an extra day a week, that's impossible. In reality, you don't need to; all you have to do is get up an extra 30 minutes earlier, just 2 or 3 mornings a week and go out for your run then. A quick 20 minute run, followed by a shower and you'll be set up to take on the rest of your day... simple!

11. NEED AN EMERGENCY ENERGY BOOSTER?

There'll always be occasions when you feel a little low on energy and the last thing you'll want to do is go out for a run, but what if there was something you could eat that would boost your energy levels within just a few minutes? Well there is and here's what you need to do to make it.

BANANA AND PEANUT TURBO BOOST

Peel a banana and chop it roughly into a bowl, add a heaped tablespoon of peanut butter and a level tablespoon of pure maple syrup (not the stuff that's got added sugar). Mix together thoroughly and heat in a microwave until warmed through. Eat and enjoy.

You should eat this at least 30 minutes before you set off, but if this doesn't give you a quick and healthy energy boost then nothing will!

12. STRENGTHEN YOUR CORE

Your core muscles which are all the muscles around your trunk (abs, obliques, erector spinae, transversus etc.) are the ones that help you to maintain an upright posture and help you to balance and run tall. If these muscles are weak, you run the risk of posture related injuries- not only to the low back, but also other joints in your body.

You need to include 5 – 10 minutes of core work up to four times a week. You can incorporate things like abdominal crunches, oblique curl ups, plank and side plank, bridge, prone cobra and back extensions - to name just a few.

13. DIP YOUR TOE IN THE WATER BEFORE DIVING IN

If you love the idea of entering a race and building up your fitness so you can run one comfortably, but are still a little unsure and undecided if it's right for you, why not volunteer as a race marshal at one of your local races? Race organisers always need more marshals and will be delighted to have your help.

To find out about the races near you, the best bet is to get in touch with local running clubs. The clubs will be able to point you in the right direction if they don't run their own events. To find out your nearest running club, simply open up Google or Bing and type in your home town followed by the keywords 'running clubs' – 'your town here - running clubs.'

Once you've witnessed first-hand the determination and sheer joy on the runners faces as they complete their races, you'll know if it's right for you or not.

14. EXCESS JIGGLE IS NO GIGGLE

No, I'm not talking about what you think I'm talking about here! I'm referring to the jiggle and rattle of loose change in your pockets when you run. It'll be irritating for both you and your running buddy as you clock up the miles, so don't carry loose change or keys in your pockets. Instead take paper money, your phone or card with you and remove the rest of your keys. Just take your house or car key - whichever you need first.

It's a very good habit to take your 'bus fare home' or a method of payment with you whenever you run just in case of any unforeseen problems. The jingle, jangle of loose change or keys will only get on your nerves - rather like the sound of a dripping tap.

15. DEALING WITH A STITCH

A stitch is a common runner's problem where the diaphragm goes into cramp or spasm. The diaphragm is a large muscle which lies between your lungs and abdominal muscles and is responsible for controlling your breathing action. One theory is that the reason for the spasm is due to a lack of blood to the area. Another line of thought is that it is due to the increased load placed on the diaphragm by the attached organs. The reason why most people get the pain on the right side is because of the weight of the liver - the heaviest of the human organs.

Many beginners suffer from regular stitches because their core muscles haven't yet developed the strength needed to minimise the bounce caused by running. Also, stitches can be made far worse by eating too close to the start of training.

To treat a stitch, the most effective action is to stop until the cramp or pain subsides. Alternatively, you can try slowing down both your speed and breathing rate and holding your stomach with your hand to limit the amount of movement there. If this doesn't work, you can try one of these breathing techniques:

- Try to alter your breathing pattern so that you breathe out when the foot of the pain–free side contacts the ground and then breathe out again the next time that foot hits the ground.
- Deep breathing is also a very effective way to deal with a stitch. To do this, you'll need to stop running I'm afraid. Once you're stationary, raise both arms above your head and slow down your breathing so you take fewer breaths that are both deeper and slower. Bending over can also slightly improve things. Try this for around a minute and then set off running slowly again.

16. RUN AT THE SAME TIME EVERY DAY

Routines can indeed be boring sometimes, which is why it is good idea to change them occasionally. Having said that, they can also motivate you. Think about the times in school when you'd set a specific time to study. Your body and mind would automatically get in the mood to study when you got close to that time.

The same thing applies to running. If you run at the same time every day, then your body will remember this action. It may fight it at first, but eventually, it will become something natural. Therefore, when you get near your usual running time, your body will know and will start preparing itself. You'll feel much more motivated to get the job done.

17. RUN YOUR TRAINING ROUTE IN REVERSE

Many people have the same running route every day. Sometimes, it's because it's easier. Other times, it's because they have no other choice. That being said, running in the same direction every time can seem dull, taking away your motivation. It's boring, and very often, you don't feel like going on a run just to see the same things over and over again.

A good and simple way to bring motivation back into the picture is to take the same route and run it in reverse. You'll cover the same time and distance, but it will feel like you are doing a different route. This is because you'll be looking at your route from a new angle.

Plus, depending on your route, it may come with different challenges and physical advantages. For instance, let's say that your regular route has you running down many hills. Now you'll be climbing them instead, which will definitely be a new challenge.

18. MAKE THE MOST OF SUNNY/DAYLIGHT HOURS

Have you noticed how you feel more motivated to run or exercise when you are in the middle of your workday? The sun is up, and you feel like you have the entire day in front of you. However, when evening comes, you don't even feel like lifting a finger, let alone to start running.

A good way to stay motivated is to take advantage of daylight hours. Instead of planning your runs in the evening, after you finish work, try doing them in the morning or during your lunch break. It may mean that you'll have to wake up earlier; but the early morning sunshine will give you a motivational boost. Running in the morning is also recommended as it will raise your energy levels for the rest of the day.

As an alternative, if you don't want to run in the morning, you can try running during your lunch break. This can be good if you have a longer lunch break. If you work a slightly flexible schedule, you may be able to work through your lunch hour and finish work an hour earlier, this will let you enjoy a run in the late afternoon sunshine.

19. TAKE YOUR RUN THROUGH NATURE

When you run through natural scenery, it will reduce your stress levels while giving you a 'feel good' boost, as it often lifts you emotionally. Not only does this make you look forward to the run, but it also keeps you running longer.

Rather than running up and down the streets, try running through woodland or a park instead. If you have a national park nearby, take advantage of the great outdoors. You can catch the bus to that location if you are far from it - as long as the nature run itself is long enough for you to meet your fitness goals.

Running in a natural setting can also give you additional benefits, which will keep you on the run for longer. For example, if you don't want to run because it's hot outside, the coolness and shade of a leafy wood or forest can bring you some extra comfort.

20. IDENTIFY YOUR 'WHY'

When you start a running routine, you need to determine exactly '*why*' you are running. What's the thing that keeps you going in the first place? If you don't have a reason why you are running, it may be difficult for you to stay motivated.

Some people run because they want to increase their stamina. Others want to burn enough calories to fit back into their old jeans. Some may run for a charitable cause that they care about. If you have a vision of your long-term goal, it will be much easier for you to stick to your plan and stay motivated.

21. MAKE YOUR BED IN THE MORNING BEFORE A RUN

Getting straight out of bed and into running shoes is something that most runners do. It's a good trick, as it gives you less time to change your mind. However, the temptation of an unmade bed will still be there. Even if you are in your running gear, you may decide to stay in bed for "*just a few more minutes*." If you do that, the chances are very high that you will fall back to sleep.

A better idea is to make your bed the moment you wake up. We know that it's an extra drag, but you'll be less tempted to lie down on your freshly made bed. You'll have no other option than to go out the door and start running - which ensures that you complete your daily running goal.

22. KEEP YOUR RUNS FOR THE MORNING

While there's nothing wrong with running in the evening; you're better off setting your runs for the morning if possible. You will be on your feet all day – so, in the evening, there is a higher chance that your feet will be swollen or tired. This could significantly lower your performance as you run.

Moreover, do bear in mind that running is a form of cardiovascular exercise and any sort of cardio will kick your adrenaline into a higher drive. If you run in the evening, the chances are that it could keep you up at night. On the other hand, if you run in the morning, it'll give you the energy you need throughout the day. Also, your feet will feel fresher in the morning.

23. LISTEN TO SOMETHING NEW DURING YOUR RUN

You probably have a playlist that you already use during your run, packed with the same songs that amp you up every time! It's a good thing because you know they will keep you going. However, as much as this music can put you in a good mood and give you energy, it can still become dull after some time. This will cause you to relax into a rhythm, preventing you from pushing beyond your comfort zone.

This is why you might want to listen to a new music or albums on your run. If your favorite band just released a new album, don't listen to it just yet. Keep it for your next run! Not only will this make you more motivated for this run, but hearing the new songs will amp you up even more. You will be so pulled into the music that you won't realise you've completed the distance. Make sure that you run in a safe place if you're planning on listening to music as you run.

24. CONSIDER RUNNING AT NIGHT FOR A CHANGE

OK, we already mentioned morning runs are a great thing, but for night owls, night runs can be more convenient and sometimes more effective. When you run in the morning, the chances are high that you will run alongside bikes, cars, pedestrians – and overall, many other people waking up. Mornings are often very busy, which means you are not likely to find the peace and tranquility of an empty street.

Things are different in the evening. There are fewer cars and not too many pedestrians either. You can run on the track or pavement without having to slow down for other people. This can help you improve - especially if you are running for a set length of time. Just ensure that you're running in a safe area and that you are always on a well-lit path.

25. DON'T DRINK TOO MUCH WATER BEFORE A RUN

You need to drink some water before and during your run that's for sure, but you must keep it to a minimum. You may feel tempted to down one or two cups of water before your run so that you don't have to drink during your run. However, do keep it to small amounts, giving it time to absorb. 3-5 fluid ounces in regular intervals should be enough.

For one, drinking too much water before a run can make you want to go to the loo quicker than usual. Secondly, the sloshing sound in your stomach will be an extra annoyance to deal with. Thirdly - and most importantly- too much water can cause your blood sodium level to drop. As your kidneys won't be able to remove the excess water, your body can begin to swell. Not only could this slow down your progress, but it may also affect your health.

26. TREAT YOUR FEET TO A MASSAGE

When you start running, your heart rate increases in order to send more blood to your working muscles. When this happens, your feet get ignored, as blood is flowing in limited amounts and being diverted away to more important parts of your body. This puts you at risk of foot cramps or other potential injuries as you run. With the blood circulation in them being low, your feet can also feel very sore after the run.

A good way to prevent this is to give your feet a massage once you get home. This will help to relieve soreness while improving blood circulation. You can do this yourself, by applying pressure with your own hands, or you may choose to use a foot massager. If you massage your feet regularly- after or even before a run- the blood vessels in your feet will begin to open up. The oxygenated blood will flow more easily through your body, preventing cramps and swelling from occurring.

27. LEARN TO BREATHE CORRECTLY

When you're running, you need to breathe using the same rhythm as your body. The inhale and exhale ratio will pretty much depend on the intensity of your exercise, so you need to follow your rhythm. Listen to your body as you are running.

A GOOD TIP: Breathe in for three strikes of your feet and breathe out for two of them. If you are sprinting or running at a faster pace, use the 2:1 breathing pattern. If you don't know what rhythm you are using , simply pay attention to your breathing and your body. Find a breathing pattern you feel comfortable with and stick with it.

28. LAY OUT YOUR RUNNING CLOTHES NEXT TO YOU

One good way to make sure you don't skip your run is to lay your clothes right next to you. This is very useful if you plan your runs in the morning, as you can get dressed the moment you wake up. There is less time for you to change your mind! you'll no longer be rummaging for your running gear. Some people just give up on clothes hunting and go back to sleep.

That being said, when you set out everything right next to you, it will act as a reminder of what you are supposed to do. As a beginner runner, you may forget why you set your alarm in the morning. However, when you open your eyes and see your running clothes, you'll remember! Moreover, you'll be more tempted to work out if only to avoid the hassle of putting everything back into the wardrobe!

29. DON'T FORGET TO STRETCH

Many runners, especially those going on early runs literally start running the moment they put on their shoes. This allows them to finish their routine in record time and get on with the rest of their day. Having said this, not stretching before a workout can be the worst thing that you can do for your muscles.

Stretching helps your muscles get ready for flexing and contracting. If you don't stretch, your muscles are almost taken by surprise, and you will more likely experience aches as the day goes by. Also, the chances of injury increase, as the muscles are not fully ready to engage. This may lead to pulled or tight muscles and this will prevent you from completing your session.

When you stretch, you also improve flexibility in your muscles. Your tendons, ligaments, and muscles will be able to stretch further, increasing your strides. This will help you run greater distances every day. It takes no more than 5 minutes of stretching before every run and you're good to go.

30. RUN WITH YOUR MOUTH CLOSED

When you are running, a good tip would be to keep your mouth closed. Sure, there are instances when breathing through your mouth may feel easier – in which case, you should alternate breathing methods. Still, your brain gets more oxygen if you breathe through your nose. Breathing through the mouth can also cause your throat to feel dry, prompting you to stop for more water breaks.

Moreover, when you keep your mouth closed as you are running, your lungs will naturally take deeper breaths. The diaphragm will be used just in the way it's intended to, so you will not have to force your breathing. Even if you're used to breathing through your mouth, your body will naturally adjust to breathing through your nose.

Plus, think about the bugs you risk swallowing as you run. By keeping your mouth closed, you stay away from unwanted "snacks". Running through the city will also expose you to pollution, which will go straight into your throat. When you keep your mouth closed, you prevent yourself from ingesting a variety of harmful contaminants as your nose has a much better filter than your mouth.

31. RELAX YOUR SHOULDERS

During your runs, you should get into the habit of relaxing your shoulders. If you keep your shoulders tense, then your upper back and neck will have the same tension. This can significantly alter your posture and impact the motion of your arms. You do not want this while you are running.

Your arms are there to offer you rhythm, balance, and power. By not relaxing your shoulders, you prevent yourself from running properly. It will also make you tire more quickly, which can affect your progress and shorten your distances. Next time you go on a run, remember that relaxing doesn't make you weaker; it keeps you going for longer.

32. TRY SOME SCENIC OR PRETTY TRAFFIC- FREE ROUTES

As a runner, you're probably not really bothered about the route you take, as long as you can complete the distance. You just put on your shoes and then start jogging or running on the pavement. However, for a better run, you should find a safer, traffic-free route. Instead of running in the city centre, try a forest path or an area of green space.

When you run in areas with lots of traffic, you'll have less control over when you can slow down or pick your pace up again. The traffic will decide – and depending on the area, the buildings can be dull and boring. Instead find a visually appealing route where you won't have to slow your pace down for traffic.

It doesn't necessarily have to be a natural park or forest – a pretty and quiet neighbourhood will also do the trick. Does your city have a neighbourhood with more tree-lined streets, or perhaps some pretty architectural buildings? If so, try doing your runs there. It will be much more satisfying to run in a place that you enjoy, without the hooting of car horns to distract you.

33. START EVERY RUN AT A SLOW PACE

You may feel tempted to set off at a fast pace from the very beginning of your run, thinking that it'll save you time and allow you to finish your run much faster. The problem is that when you start running, you may not be properly warmed up. As a result, you may tire much faster than expected or even pull a muscle.

Go into every run with the mindset that you'll finish strong. When you are getting closer to the end, then run your fastest and give it your all. But when you start, do it at a slow pace. It will help warm up your muscles and gradually increase your heart rate. This way, you won't end up huffing and puffing by the time you get to the finish line.

34. DON'T FEEL BAD IF YOU MISS A DAY

Most of the time, when you run, you like to stick to the schedule you created and that's a good thing, so when you miss a day, you feel bad

– as if that one day is going to set you back. Here's a news flash: it won't. This is why you shouldn't beat yourself up if something happens and you have to miss a day.

Your body also needs time to recover- especially if you're a beginner. Going at it every day can make you feel more tired and sore than you should be. Use that day as an opportunity to rest and don't fret. When it comes to your fitness progress, one day off doesn't mean that much. What's important is to not let that missed day derail you completely – because one missed day can turn into several missed days if you're not determined enough. So, enjoy the rest day, but make sure you keep on track with your runs!

35. LEAN INTO YOUR PACE

If you've ever seen the running ninja trend on social media, you may have noticed they learn forward. The real run is not as extreme, but they are right about one thing: by leaning forward, you can improve your running speed. However, this should only be a slight lean forward, as leaning too far forward can lead to injury.

When you adopt a slight forward lean, you promote good hip extension, which can improve your strides. This lean should not start in your middle area, but rather at the ankles. This will help promote proper alignment, allowing you to keep your body in a straight line as you run.

36. KEEP YOUR KNEE HEIGHT UNDER CONTROL

When you're running, make sure that you keep your knee height under control. If you raise your knees too high, then running may turn into a bounce instead of a smooth glide over the road. Each stride you take will deliver more impact into your body and make you feel tired faster. This is one of the main factors that causes soreness in your feet, knees and hips.

Instead, keep your knee at just a slight bend. This will limit the impact that your body gets as you strike your feet on the ground. Sure, you may need a higher knee action when you are doing a running drill, but even then, it should be limited. When you lift your knees, you should also do it forwards instead of upwards to reduce the impact and increase your speed.

37. ALWAYS LOOK STRAIGHT AHEAD – NOT AT YOUR FEET

Many runners tend to look at their feet while running. However, when you look down, you can cause tension in your neck and shoulders which is something you should avoid when running. Plus, when you are looking at your feet, you'll be too focused on your own progress which can subconsciously make you tire faster.

To avoid this, try looking straight ahead. Focus on something that is around 20-30 metres ahead of you. This will take your attention off your feet, helping you to run without the associated tension. You can look at this point as a goal that you want to reach – and each time you pass one goal, you can choose another. It can make the run more enjoyable.

38. DON'T SKIP SLEEP IN FAVOUR OF RUNNING

In today's society, you want to make the most out of the 24 hours that you have. Often, this causes you to go to sleep late, after watching your favorite Netflix series and thinking that getting 4-5 hours of sleep is OK. You may be thinking your dedication makes you tough, but it may actually harm your progress.

When you're tired, your body will spend a lot of energy just trying to keep you awake. In this scenario, you can't expect it to properly burn calories and keep you running. If you want to improve the quality of your running, make sure you get at least 7-8 hours sleep every night. Find a sleep pattern that works for you, but don't sacrifice sleep just to run at a certain time, instead find a better way to manage your time.

7 CHAPTER MOTIVATIONAL **TIPS**

1. LISTEN TO MOTIVATIONAL MUSIC

As a runner, you should not underestimate the power that motivational music has over your psyche. A good, upbeat song can not only help you power through your moments of fatigue, but it can also distract you from potential exercising pain.

Since music also puts you in a better mood, it can motivate you into working out for a longer time. It increases your powers of endurance, reducing the insurmountable amount of effort needed that your brain perceives you will need to succeed.

Plus, a person listening to their favourite music cannot help but follow the tempo. Make a playlist with your most energy- inducing songs and take them on your next run with you. Leave the sad, melancholic songs at home, though. These only encourage you to sleep or relax – something you don't want on a run.

2. PUT ON YOUR RUNNING GEAR IMMEDIATELY AFTER YOU WAKE UP

The hardest part of going on a run is getting yourself out of the house in the first place. After that, once you start running, you'll be able to increase your motivation with the natural adrenaline boost you are getting through exercise. The trouble is if you just potter around the house after you get up, you still have time to change your mind and jump back into your comfy, cosy, warm bed.

This is why you should put your running gear on as soon as you wake up. Ideally after making your bed too, as it reduces your temptations. That having being said, if it doesn't, you'll still be more motivated simply by wearing your workout clothes.

After putting your running shoes on (unless you have brand-new ones) you won't be able to get back into bed with them on! If you're 'sitting on the fence' about going on a run, especially in the morning, putting your running gear on may just be the motivation!

3. SET YOUR ALARM AND PUT IT OUT OF REACH

How many times have you set up your alarm, only to accidentally sleep through it? Most of the time, it's not even your fault – you are so used to the alarm going off that you hit "snooze" right away. It barely even has time to ring before you stop the noise! This often happens because the alarm is right next to you.

The split seconds when your alarm rings are the ones you are least motivated – and the most likely time for you to go back to sleep. All you need is the opportunity to press that snooze button. This is why you need to make it impossible to do that!

A good tip is to place your alarm away from the bedside. This way, you'll have to get up and turn off the alarm. Even if you're still on the fence about running, you are more motivated than before. At least you got out of bed – and since you're already there, you might as well keep going!

4. USE MOTIVATING OR LOUD MUSIC AS AN ALARM

Here's a good tip for those lacking the motivation to wake up in the morning! Why not try a very loud or motivating alarm tone. Many people choose soothing songs just so they are woken up gradually, but there is one slight problem. These songs are so soothing, that all they do is lull you back to sleep!

Instead of going for this kind of gently coaxing alarm song, try something louder instead. Perhaps you have a quick-paced song that gets you in a motivated mood or you found an extreme alarm clock sound online that contains every single siren and bombing alert known to man! Sure, it's not as soothing as a relaxing tone and a stark way to start your day, but it will definitely get you up!

These alarms, as annoying as they may be, will set your heart rate in full motion – if only because they give you a mini heart attack every morning! You've already started your cardio, and you didn't even start running yet! Plus, the chances are that you'll be so annoyed with your alarm that you'll start running just to blow off some steam.

5. FORCE YOURSELF TO TAKE A SHOWER 'BEFORE' YOUR RUN

We know that showering after a run is a given. When you run, you sweat a lot – so if you don't shower, you'll end up stinking. Not to mention that it can lead to acne breakouts if the sweat clogs your pores. Having said this, you may want to take a shower before you start running too.

But showers take precious time in the morning, and you don't want to waste the extra minutes - especially if you prefer sleeping over showers. A cold shower can sometimes be more effective at waking you up than a cup of coffee. If simply splashing your face with cold water can revitalise you, imagine what it will do if you immerse your whole body in it!

You don't have to take a full-blown shower, with shampoo and conditioner. You can do that afterwards. Now, all you need is to step into the shower and give yourself a quick refresh. Or just use some body wash if you sweat a lot at night. This will energise you and this will help you feel more motivated for your run.

6. SET A PICTURE OF YOUR FITNESS GOALS AS A WALLPAPER/SCREENSAVER

If you're running to reach certain fitness goals or to lose weight, you might try to use a visualisation method. Only this time, use a picture. By setting it as your wallpaper, you will see it each time you check your phone or your computer, and it will remind you of your objective.

Perhaps you have a picture of yourself from a time when you looked your best. Or you have a celebrity whose physique is to your liking, and you want to look that way. As long as the goal is realistic, that picture should help motivate you.

7. USE THE 5 MINUTE RULE

We all have days when we simply don't feel like running. Perhaps we're feeling tired, or just don't want to get out of bed. That's normal, as we all have days when we're just too tired to run. Still, this could also mean that you're lazy!

To give yourself a boost you could try the 5-minute rule. Basically, what you have to do is run for 5 minutes, and then decide if you want to carry on after that. If you still don't feel like running, it means you are not up for it – at which point, you should call it a day.

Those 5 minutes will often be enough to kick-start your motivation. If you start by thinking *"I'll run for 5 minutes and then I'll see,"* you'll be less likely to skip your run completely. So, there's a good chance that you'll want to carry on.

8. TURN IT INTO A GAME

To make your run more interesting, you need to think about ways to keep your mind busy. Simply running can be very boring, but by turning it into a game, you can make it much more entertaining.

If you're running alone, you may try counting similar things you see, like dogs or how many red cars from a certain brand you pass - for example. Give a name to each dog you see, based on their appearance.

If you are running with a group, you may also try games such as *"I spy with my little eye"* or even start a game of tag to lift the spirits. You're already running after all, so it's the perfect game for you!

9. CHANGE THE TONE OF YOUR MUSIC

When you go running, you may have a playlist that you put on at all times. The same old songs worked wonders on you before, but now you're playing those tunes each time you go running. The problem is that while you may still love those tunes, they may have grown dull over time.

Music can have an amazing impact on how you perform. The trick to feeling motivated is to change the tunes from time to time. If you usually enjoy energetic DJ beats, why not try some rock songs as a change. Imagine how it will feel when Bon Jovi's *"It's My Life"* starts playing – unless it wasn't already on your playlist that is!

Obviously, you should listen to the kind of music that you like, however, the songs ideally need to be upbeat. Other than that, update your playlist regularly so that you don't get set in a rut.

10. REDUCE YOUR MINIMUM RUNNING TIME

You will likely set yourself a minimum running time. It's not a limit, but a time that you'll have to reach each day- regardless of your mood. Many runners set around 30 minutes as their standard running time, often running in sprints to maintain a good heart rate.

The problem is that when you set a higher running time as your goal, you'll be more tempted to skip a run. You'll convince yourself that you are either too tired for this or you just don't have the time. In these cases, you must remember a very common saying: that *less is more.*

Instead of setting your minimum running time for 30 minutes, try putting it at 15-20 minutes instead. This way, you won't be as likely to skip the run, simply because you have a shorter run ahead of you which will be less daunting. The chances are that even if you weren't in the mood before, your adrenaline will kick in and allow you to run more.

11. TELL FRIENDS AND FAMILY ABOUT YOUR RUNNING GOALS

Sometimes, simply telling other people about your running goals can motivate you into sticking to a routine. When you tell your friends, you're giving yourself more accountability and instinctively, you'll be driven enough to give it your best.

Some people see it's "guilt tripping you into running," to spare yourself the embarrassment if you get lazy. You already told them, so you can't excuse yourself now, right? Well, rather than focusing on this, try to see it as a beneficial boost.

When you tell others, they will root for your success and support you in reaching your goal. Announcing your goals will also make them real. When you put them into a realistic plan like that, it'll spur you on and it will be much easier for you to keep running.

12. FIND A GOOD CAUSE TO RUN FOR

Sometimes, running for an average goal doesn't help get you motivated. Your goals and priorities may change, and when you can't be bothered, you don't care if you skip a day. You'll run tomorrow, and you think that your calories along with your endurance won't suffer that much.

If you want to motivate yourself into running, find a worthwhile cause that you care about deeply instead of a goal. For instance, joining a non-profit charity run might get you out of the house. For each mile that you run, a certain sum will be given to the charity. This should keep you motivated enough to stay on track.

8 CHAPTER RACE DAY **TIPS**

1. DON'T SHOWBOAT IN YOUR NEW RUNNING KIT

It's understandable that race day is a special occasion and that you want to look and feel your best. You've trained for many weeks or months to get to this point and hopefully you've got yourself into great shape.

However something that many people do in an attempt to look a little smarter than they do in their normal running scruffs is to buy a whole new wardrobe for the occasion. Unfortunately this could be a big mistake, especially if you're running longer distances as the new gear, may rub or pull in certain places, leaving your skin irritated or sore. In the worst case scenario for example, a new pair of running socks might not give you the support or protection against blisters that you need and you could be forced to stop running altogether and miss out on completing the race.

It's a simple rule. By all means buy yourself something special for a race day, but wear it in a few times before the big day first.

2. HOLD YOURSELF BACK

With the excitement and adrenaline of the starting line, many newbie's set off far too fast in a burst of enthusiasm, only to pay for their excitement further into the race. It's a better policy to set off much slower than you think you should and then speed up as you go along. This way, you'll know that you've got something left in reserve further along the course instead of running on empty for the last few miles.

For your first race, your goal should simply be to experience the thrills and atmosphere... if it's slower than you'd normally run, who cares. You can go all out on your next race now you know what to expect.

3. TAKE A DISPOSABLE RAIN COAT

If the weather is bad and you're faced with the prospect of running most of the race in heavy rain, then you need to take a rain jacket with you. If it's hot however, you don't want to be saddled with a rain jacket and other layers to carry around with you when you start to warm up. So instead take a disposable rain coat or a large bin bag with 3 holes cut out of it - one for your head and two for your arms. This way you can throw it away later on in the race if you no longer need it.

4. DRINKING ON THE GO

When you pick up drinking cups at aid stations, it can often be quite difficult to drink from them. A simple tip to make this challenge a little easier, is to squeeze the cup gently so it folds slightly down the middle and drink from it this way. You're far more likely to get a mouthful of water as opposed to spilling most of it down your top.

5. DON'T FORGET TO LUBE UP

When you're running over any distance, there's going to be some movement in the clothes you wear. As a technique to reduce the amount of irritation on your skin you should apply liberal amounts of Vaseline or Body Glide over any areas that cause you problems.

The most common areas of friction are over the chest (guys don't forget the nipples) around the neck, between the thighs, the heels and between the toes - and anywhere else you might have problems with. Doing this is a good way to prevent blisters and chafing.

Test this out on a long training session before you use it on race day to see if you feel any benefits.

9 CHAPTER INTRODUCTION TO **NUTRITION**

Your **SUCCESS** or failure in reaching your running targets will to some extent depend on your ability to **follow** this nutritionally balanced diet consistently.

Healthy eating for runners is essentially **very easy**. You don't need to count points, calories, grams, work out percentages or nutrient ratios. You do however, need to be ORGANISED and have plenty of the right types of foods readily available.

The main reasons *most people fail* to eat a well balanced diet whilst following a running programme are due to: -

- Lack of **ORGANISATION**
- Lack of *planning*
- Lack of **understanding** the meaning of correct and balanced nutrition
- Lack of ***CONSISTENCY***

After having worked with hundreds of clients and seen their successes and their failures, I have been able to *pinpoint the reasons* why some people are very successful whilst others only do averagely well.

THE NEED FOR A BALANCED DIET

The need for a balanced diet is of **utmost importance**. If you are aiming to improve your ability to run further and faster, get into great shape or lose weight but you *don't address your diet, then you will fall short of achieving any real success.*

This is why I have devised this *fully automated* diet. It is a simple solution **to the most common problem** runner's face when training and exercising regularly.

You will see that all the meals are as **balanced** as possible without being restrictive or obsessive. The meals provide a wide array of nutrients with *minimal fats or sugars*. The plan does allow for TREAT FOODS though and the odd luxury.

My aim is to make eating to **support your running achievable** by supplying recipes which provide healthy and supportive meals or snacks, give *superb results* and an ongoing supply of necessary and essential nutrients. You will notice all the meals have a balanced feel, are low in fat and relatively quick and easy to prepare.

Basically speaking sweets, chocolate, crisps, pastries and other highly processed foods don't have a role to play in a typical healthy diet...if you are trying to improve your fitness or lose weight whilst *still* eating this type of food, *you will become despondent* very quickly. By switching to wholesome, fresh foods you will begin to feel the effect of having loads more energy, endurance, confidence, a visible and improved condition of your hair and skin and an improved digestive system. Wholesome foods also do one other vital job...*They make you feel fuller for longer.*

For an eating plan or system of nutrition to be successful it must be SIMPLE AND EASY to follow

The **Runners Guide To Nutrition** is as easy and quick as humanly possible.

It is just not possible to get the balance and the right amount of vitamins, minerals and nutrients you need from packet and processed foods, so these have generally been avoided in this plan.

There is a **minimum** of preparation involved, but obviously for you to eat well *you need to be in control* of the foods you eat and by making or preparing them yourself then this is the best way to ensure this happens.

Having said that there are many *easy food solutions* these days that address the problems of **lack of time** or interest in food preparation. Most supermarkets now sell pre- prepared salads and vegetables in single portion sized bags for example.

Ready prepared fresh fruit salads are available in some stores which takes away the effort of preparing them...rice cakes, yogurts and cottage cheese are all examples of **very quick and easy snack foods** and many more are listed in the menu section.

If possible try to do a weekly shop following the simple shopping lists given for each week. The lists ensure that all the foods, ingredients and herbs etc. you require for the week are bought and are readily available to you. Doing this simplifies the whole process and makes it much more unlikely that you will get caught short with none of the right types of food available to eat.

In this healthy eating plan I recommend you choose only *one treat day* each week to have a couple of the sorts of foods you enjoy that aren't particularly good for you, don't go mad but don't feel guilty either.

Alcohol is a **no-no** during the week, but if you like an occasional drink then a couple at the weekend won't affect your training too much. Just remember all things in moderation but if you have a long run planned the next day, don't drink at all.

You will find a section on the importance of water, which outlines the **key reasons** for its use. Water is not mentioned in the menu section as I am expecting you to drink it throughout the day at regular intervals.

MONITOR BOTH YOUR WEIGHT AND MEASUREMENTS EVERY WEEK

With regards to portion sizes, you shouldn't worry about this too much to begin with, just monitor your hips, waist and weight measurements each week...if these are static or coming down, then you are eating the correct amount.

As a general rule, *EAT WHEN HUNGRY, STOP WHEN FULL*. Don't just keep eating to empty the plate...listen to when your body is telling you that you are full.

On training days you will need to consume more carbohydrates such as pasta, rice, potatoes, bananas etc. to allow for replenishing the glycogen stores in your muscles which will have been depleted through your training.

Also there is a need for extra proteins to be consumed such as fish, chicken and turkey - soon after exercise because of the role that this nutrient plays in renewing and repairing the damage caused to muscle tissue through muscular contractions.

PLEASE NOTE...If you are aiming to reduce your body weight and lose fat whilst training, there will be a chance of gaining weight if you don't balance the amount of food you eat each day with the amount of calories you burn off through exercise.

You will generally have an increased appetite after exercise and may over-eat at these times.

You will see that the diet has been based on **low-fat** sources of protein such as fish and Quorn. This is because fish supplies essential omega 3 fatty acids and is generally very low in fat.

However *chicken and turkey can also be used* in any of the meals to replace fish or Quorn.

As much as possible avoid using red meats because they are very high in saturated fats.

REGULAR GRAZING HELPS TO MAINTAIN A HIGHER METABOLIC RATE

You may well find that *eating at such regular intervals is difficult* to do, you may not always feel like eating. There are two reasons I ask you to do this. Firstly, the body will be constantly supplied with nutrients to assist in **repair and recovery** and secondly, ***regular grazing helps to maintain a higher metabolic rate***.

Obviously the chances of you liking all the foods and meals contained in the menu sheets are very slim. **Don't worry about it**...simply replace with foods you do like.

For example you may choose to replace Quorn with minced turkey when you are preparing Quorn chilli and rice. You may not like butternut squash soup and so may decide to make your own soup instead. I have given you plenty of alternatives on page 8.

As much as possible try to stick to the planned meals, or plan out your own menu and select foods with similar properties. What you **MUSTN'T** do is skip the fruit and vegetables in the diet...these are *ESSENTIAL* to your success.

Fruit and vegetables will supply essential vitamins, minerals and water, will fill you up and stop you from having cravings and turning to sugary and fatty snacks.

If you do find yourself replacing foods in the menu that's fine, just ensure you are **not replacing them with processed alternatives**. All the main meals should ideally be prepared from scratch with fresh ingredients and using minimal fats and sugars.

FOOD REPLACEMENT GUIDE

I **strongly** advise you choose foods you **enjoy** that also fall into the *low-fat, low sugar, unprocessed category* ...don't try to force down foods you just don't like.

If you do need to buy any frozen ready meals, these should be eaten as a ***rarity*** and not a staple to your diet. Eating these **WILL** affect the *speed of your progress* and you will also have no control over their contents.

Don't forget the foods in this manual have been selected for a number of reasons, including balance, their **nutrient content and variety**. It is so important to ***plan in advance***, so if you are going to replace foods of your own preference then do so at the start of the plan and write them into the menus and shopping lists.

In the table below, the *recommended* foods in the plan appear on the left of the table and alternatives to these on the right. So go ahead and make your selections if you need to and try to **enjoy the foods you select**.

RECOMMENDED FOODS	ALTERNATIVES
Porridge, muesli	Shredded Wheat, Cornflakes, Weetabix
Semi-skimmed milk	Skimmed milk, soya milk
Quorn	Turkey, chicken, lean mince
Low–fat yoghurt	Low-fat fromage frais
Cottage cheese	Low–fat soft cheese (use sparingly)
Salmon, tuna, monkfish, mackerel	Any other fish, chicken or turkey
Houmous	Tomato salsa, cottage cheese
Raisins and sunflower seeds	Any unsweetened dried fruits and nuts or seeds
Pitta bread	Wholemeal bread, rice cakes, breadsticks

You can also replace foods within the plan with each other...for example instead of tuna salad, you may decide to have salmon or chicken salad instead. Use common sense when replacing foods in the plan, try to select similar foods...for example vegetables replaced with other vegetables. Fish replaced with other fish or poultry.

WATER

AIM TO DRINK 2 LITRES OF WATER EVERY DAY

Drinking this amount of water each day ensures that a number of things happen:

- Nutrients are more easily transported around the body.
- The digestive system is lubricated, and correct body temperature is maintained.

- *Toxins are removed* from the body. These are often stored just below the surface of the skin in the form of cellulite and other fatty tissues.
- Fluids lost through everyday activities (and more especially during exercise) can be **replaced immediately** - thereby avoiding dehydration.
- Total levels of **body fat** are *reduced* because water thins out the fatty acids which are used in the body for energy or if not needed immediately, stored for future use.
- **Dehydration is avoided** which can cause the metabolism to slow down. The opposite is also true because when there is adequate water in the body, the metabolism is speeded up.

Water is **the most essential substance** needed by the body...thirst should not be used as an indicator of fluid status because at this point you are *probably already dehydrated*...Do not wait until you are thirsty before you drink.

Water, milk and sugar-free drinks can all be counted as part of your daily water consumption. Fruit juices and sugary drinks are termed as *HYPERTONIC* – this means they have a higher concentration of sugar than the blood and therefore can not be absorbed into the blood stream to assist in maintaining normal fluid levels.

TOP TIP - Try keeping a 2 litre bottle of water in the fridge and drink from this each day to ensure you are **drinking the correct amount**.

Alternatively keep a few ½ litre bottles in the fridge, car, bedroom etc. This ensures there is always water on hand and acts as a gentle reminder.

As an alternative to plain tap or bottled water, try adding ice, lemon or lime to give a *refreshing alternative*. The occasional use of carbonated water also gives an added twist.

Check flavoured water has no added sugar and drink occasionally as an alternative.

FRUITS AND VEGETABLES

Aim to eat at least *5 portions of fruit and vegetables every day*, these portions could include any fresh fruit and vegetables, frozen or tinned as long as they are tinned in fruit juice or water, **avoid items** preserved in syrup or brine (salted water).

Frozen fruit and vegetables may even have more nutritional benefit than their fresh alternatives because these items are usually frozen within two hours of harvesting. Therefore the maximum nutrients and **vitamins they contain are frozen in them**.

Fruit and vegetables are extremely high in vitamins, essential minerals, water and fibre and are therefore essential for health and well-being.

The *digestive system will not function properly* without **adequate fibre** which is found in many fruits and vegetables as well as other foods.

Skin quality is poor with the exclusion of certain vitamins and the whole body does not effectively utilise the nutrients in the foods consumed if the correct quantity of these essential elements are not present.

FRUITS ARE AN EXCELLENT WAY OF SNACKING THROUGHOUT THE DAY...

Fruits are quick and convenient to eat and relatively cheap. By ensuring you always have a full and varied fruit bowl on hand you can help encourage healthy snacking.

Aim to try new fruits as these may surprise you and because each fruit has a *different combination of nutrients* you can fully ensure that you are consuming the widest range of vitamins and minerals.

Balancing correctly your levels of vitamins, minerals and fibre can have a much greater effect on your current weight levels. You will find you are more capable of stabiliising your weight or losing or gaining weight whichever is your aim.

YOUR BODY WILL BE MORE RESPONSIVE BECAUSE IT IS FUNCTIONING EFFECTIVELY.

Fruit salads served with yogurt or low-fat crème fraiche are a tasty alternative to most other sugar laden sweets and desserts. **Vegetables and salads** can be readily eaten as an accompaniment to most meals or they can *form the basis* of the meal itself.

Roasted vegetables are a tasty alternative to chips and much healthier and surprisingly easy to prepare. Simply select a variety of vegetables (take into account their various cooking times, some may need to be added to the roasting tin later) scrub their skins (these are usually where most of the goodness is stored) - or peel if you prefer- drizzle in olive oil, making sure each piece has a thin coating, add herbs and spices to the mix and bake at the top of the oven at gas mark 7 or 220'c until slightly soft.

CARBOHYDRATES

Carbohydrates should provide the body with at least 60% of its total daily calories, The main use of carbohydrates in the in body is to provide us with energy.

When carbohydrates enter the body they are always converted to glucose before being used by the cells.

Glucose is the **only source of energy** that the brain can use.

In terms of satisfying carbohydrate needs, there is **no difference** between simple and complex carbohydrates.

The difference is that a potato (complex carbohydrates) will fill you up where as a few spoonfuls of sugar (simple carbohydrates) will leave you *feeling empty and wanting more very quickly.*

Complex carbohydrates (especially in their natural form) can also provide the diet with protein, fibre, vitamins and minerals, *none of which* can be found in sugar.

Sugar *provides empty calories* and a continued over-consumption of sugars can lead to maturity onset diabetes (Type 2 Diabetes) and can cause dental decay.

It is quite **difficult to over-consume calories** from complex carbohydrate sources because you will usually *feel full first*. However if you do over- consume calories over and above your daily requirements from whichever source be it proteins, fats OR carbohydrates, the excess **will be stored** on the body as fat.

The difference being an over-consumption of 300 fat calories leads to storage of 300 kcals of body fat whereas an over-consumption of 300 kcals from carbohydrates will lead to storage of about 230kcals of body fat. This is because it actually **takes some energy** for the body to convert the carbohydrates to body fat.

In the past bread, potatoes, pasta and other starchy foods were avoided by dieters who considered them to be the most fattening foods.

This poor **image of carbohydrates is incorrect** and comes from the fact that most of these foods are usually served with cream sauces and added fats etc.

Complex carbohydrates in the diet should be **increased**, whereas simple carbohydrates should be *decreased.*

Eating a diet high in complex carbohydrates (high fibre) will make you feel fuller sooner, which may reduce total calorie consumption.

Generally speaking the nearer the food is to its natural state when eaten, the more nutritional benefit there is likely to be.

These high fibre, nutrient dense foods are also usually much lower in fat than animal derived foods.

Complex carbohydrates *provide dietary bulk or fibre*, which leaves us **feeling full** and *assists the efficient working of the digestive system.*

Fibre is mainly found in the outer wall of foods and is therefore higher in those foods which are unrefined.

THERE ARE TWO MAIN TYPES OF FIBRE, SOLUBLE AND INSOLUBLE

Insoluble fibre does not dissolve in water in the stomach and cleanses the digestive system, preventing illnesses such as constipation, haemorrhoids and diverticulosis (blow outs of the intestinal wall).

Soluble fibre dissolves in water in the stomach and this digestive process can help to lower cholesterol levels.

Current adult recommendations are 30 grams of fibre to be eaten each day.

There are 4 calories per gram of carbohydrate- a simple or complex carbohydrate.

SUGAR

Refined sugar can be found in a **huge amount of products** these days from drinks to soups to bread to make their taste more attractive. This simple addition to foods can have a disastrous affect on your weight loss efforts.

Sugar does not just refer to the type added to tea or coffee for example but *any refined sugar or type of sugars*.

One of the most important changes we can make to our diet is to **cut down or ideally cut out totally our intake of refined carbohydrates - especially simple sugars**.

These sugars can be found in many things including cakes, buns, sweets, processed foods etc.

The main problem with sugary foods is they *stop the body from burning* fat as fuel - something that we don't want to happen.

We all have the **potential to burn fat even while resting**, but this will never happen if a diet comprises of regular helpings of foods containing sugars.

What basically happens is that whenever you eat sugar it causes a rapid spike in blood sugar levels and this in turn sends signals to the brain to produce insulin to **remove the sugar from the blood** and take it to the muscles to be stored or used for energy.

The problem is that whenever insulin is produced to do this task the production of glucagon stops.

Glucagon is the hormone responsible for **taking fat from the cells** to the muscles to burn as energy and therefore when this hormone is suppressed you *will not burn fat at all because you physically can't.* So if you are exercising on a regular basis and trying to lose weight, but not seeing any visible results this may be part of the reason.

Eating excess sugar has the following effects:

- Stops the ability of the body to burn fat as fuel
- Causes highs in blood sugar levels leading to the excess production of insulin
- High blood sugar and insulin can increase the storage of fat
- Continued over use of sugar can lead to Type 2 diabetes when your body continues to produce too much insulin which may eventually lead to obesity and heart problems – amongst others.
- Causes lows in blood sugar levels creating sugar cravings and extreme hunger pangs
- Consumption of extra sugar laden calories with no nutritional benefit

The taste of sweetness is a pleasure, *a liking for it is totally natural.* However, dietary guidelines recommend that we **use concentrated sugars** only in **moderation**.

Follow the guidelines below:

- Use less of all sugars, including white, brown and raw sugar, honey and syrups

- Eat less of foods containing large amounts of sugar, such as soft drinks, sweets, ice cream, cakes and biscuits.
- Select fresh fruits, frozen or fruits canned without sugar or syrup to satisfy your urge for sweets.
- Read ingredient lists on food labels to find out sugar content, if the word sucrose, glucose, maltose, dextrose, fructose or syrup appear high on the list of ingredients then the food is high in sugar. Any foods where these sweeteners appear in the first three ingredients listed should be avoided or used sparingly.

The more processed a food is, the *more likely it is to contain sugar.* Always check food labels and be wary of manufacturers breaking down sugars in order to make the product appear less sweet.

ONE FINAL NOTE – whilst fruit is very good for you, providing vitamins, minerals, fibre and a low calorie snack it does also contain natural fruit sugars which have the same affect as any other sugar.

From a purist's weight loss point of view, fruit should be limited or eaten with other foods to slow down the absorption into the blood stream.

FATS

WHAT YOU NEED, WHAT YOU DON'T

Dietary sources of fat include oils, butter, margarine, shortening, lard, meats, nuts, mayonnaise, gravy, cheese, ice cream and whole milk.

Even if you wanted to, it would be **virtually impossible** to remove all the fat from your diet because at least a trace of fat is found in almost all foods.

Fat is a valuable nutrient, in fact some fats are absolutely essential and must be present in the diet in order to maintain good health.

The essential fats are the ***omega 3 and 6 oils*** that can be found in fish, rapeseed and primrose oils. It is for this reason that *eating fish is recommended at least twice a week.*

THE ROLE OF FATS IN THE BODY

Fats perform a number of important roles in the body:

- Body fat serves as an **energy reserve** – the body can carry 30 – 50 pounds of fat (13.6- 22.6 kg)and still appear slim.
- Each of those pounds can give us about 3,500 kcals of energy.
- **Nourishes the skin, hair and muscles**
- *Insulates the body* against extremes of temperatures
- Allows the body to use and store the fat–soluble vitamins – A, D, E, K
- Provides a cushion to the internal vital organs

In women, a healthy fat intake maintains correct oestrogen levels which can be low in women on low-fat diets giving an increased risk of bone disease.

CURRENT DIETARY FAT RECOMMENDATIONS

Current intakes of fat are estimated to account for an average of 40% of our daily calorie consumption, this should be lowered to no more than 25 - 30%.

CHOLESTEROL

Cholesterol is not strictly speaking a fat but acts very much like one. Again this substance is **needed by our bodies**, so much so that the body actually makes it itself.

Cholesterol in the diet doesn't actually increase blood cholesterol levels but a *diet high in saturated fat does.*

High cholesterol levels can lead to an increased risk of coronary heart disease.

SATURATED FATS

Saturated fats are usually *solid at room temperature* and mainly come from *animal sources.*

Eating high amounts of saturated fats can lead to two main health risks - obesity and heart disease.

We should ensure that the **majority of our fat intake** is from the unsaturated types (polyunsaturated and monounsaturated).

Another type of fat to **avoid is hydrogenated fat**. This type of fat has been chemically altered by the addition of hydrogen in order for the fat to solidify making it more usable.

EAT MAINLY UNSATURATED FATS

Restrict saturated fats to no more than 25% of daily fat intake

Total fat intake should be *no more than* 25 - 30% of the daily calorie intake.

There are 9 calories per gram of fat (28g = 1 oz).

PROTEIN

Protein is *essential for the growth and maintenance* of the body's tissues and cells.

Protein is present in **most - if not all- living cells** and the constant renewal and repairing of the body's tissues means you need to eat protein regularly.

Proteins are made up of 20 **AMINO ACIDS** that all play a part in the structure of protein molecules. Amino acids can be classified into *two categories*: -

Essential – of which there are eight and these can't be made by the body, therefore they need to be eaten

Non Essential – of which there are 12, all of which can be produced by the body..

It is important that the body has a regular supply of these essential amino acids. Most people who eat a balanced diet including fish, dairy and meat should automatically be consuming enough protein as these foods are termed *COMPLETE* proteins.

Anyone on a restricted diet such as vegans, vegetarians or fruitarians will *have to work much harder* to ensure they are eating enough of these types of proteins.

For anyone not eating fish, meat or dairy products they must rely on **combining foods together** to provide a complete source of protein such as: -

Cereal grains or rice combined with legumes (beans and peas etc)

CEREAL GRAINS	LEGUMES	COMBINATIONS
Barley	Beans	Rice cakes with peanut butter
Oats	Lentils	Lentil casserole with rice
Pasta	Peas	Soya and vegetable stir fry with noodles
Rice	Peanuts	Porridge with soya milk
Wheat	Soy Products	Tacos with Chilli and salad

Protein is **vital for supporting the body** but it is *not needed* for the role of energy production, this is the job of carbohydrates and fats. Although if required it can provide a *reserve energy supply*, usually only used in **extreme circumstances** such as endurance events or in times of severe malnutrition.

As a runner you should aim to consume approximately 15 – 20% of your daily calories from lean protein sources. The more miles you run each week, the more you will need to eat, possibly up to at total of 20% of your daily calories.

There are 4 calories per gram of protein.

ALCOHOL

Alcohol is a **drug and a diuretic** because it changes the way the body functions, causing increased water excretion thereby affecting the internal water balance and ultimately weight loss or stability of weight is much harder to achieve.

Alcohol affects every organ in the body, but has the greatest effect on the liver whose job it is to convert the alcohol into energy. Liver cells can become less effective and long term overuse of alcohol can lead to liver disease.

Alcohol is NOT a stimulant; it numbs the sensory part of the brain by sedating the inhibitory nerves making us feel less tense or self conscious. **Ultimately alcohol acts as a depressan**t because it sedates all the nerve cells.

Alcohol alters the mood, helping people to relax, reducing their inhibitions and encouraging social behaviour.

When your stomach is full, the alcohol has less chance of reaching the stomach walls and being absorbed into the bloodstream and going to the brain. The opposite is true that when the stomach is empty, alcohol is absorbed much more quickly into the bloodstream.

Alcohol leads to *dehydration through frequent urination* and this in turn leads to feelings of thirst. What do most people do when they feel thirsty? The answer is they drink, but when out socially, it is very likely that the liquid chosen will not be water.

Water is the only fluid that can effectively relieve dehydration.

One of the biggest risks in consuming alcohol is the addition of extra calories with no nutritional benefit – alcohol is high in empty calories.

These calories will usually be stored as increased body fat.

Alcohol affects every tissue's ability to metabolise nutrients.

Alcohol is treated as a VIP in that the body gives it priority of metabolisation. Vitamins and minerals can not be as easily absorbed and many are excreted by the kidneys leaving the body to attempt to function without all the essential nutrients

Alcohol slows the metabolism down therefore reducing the body's ability to burn off calories.

CAFFEINE

Caffeine is a drug, which affects the central nervous system. It is both a **stimulant and a diuretic**, which amongst other things increases heart rate, boosts urine production and *raises the metabolic rate.*

It is a compound which is found in coffee beans, cola drinks, nuts, cocoa beans and tea leaves.

Being a diuretic, caffeine flushes water out of the cells of the body and into the bloodstream, into the kidneys and finally out of the system through urination.

This whole process puts more stress on the kidneys and on the heart.

Consuming diuretics will *lead to dehydration* because the internal water balance has been altered This state of dehydration makes the body **less efficient** in a number of ways, but most importantly for runners, it affects the ability to run and makes the body *less effective at burning off calories.*

Another downside to consuming a lot of caffeine is that it hinders the body's ability to absorb certain vitamins needed **to metabolise carbohydrates**, iron and calcium.

A lack of the mineral calcium can greatly affect women if they do not consume enough.

If **women** consume **low levels of calcium** (found in dairy products, some green vegetables and certain types of fish) but they also **consume caffeine regularly,** this may lead to a much greater risk of *developing bone disease.*(such as osteoporosis)

This is due to the fact that the caffeine has prevented the small amounts of calcium consumed from being absorbed into the bloodstream and has laid them down as calcium salts on the outer layer of the bones instead.

Caffeine can build up in the system over a period of time because the body can't metabolise it very effectively and therefore it gets stored.

Too much caffeine can cause anxiety, restlessness, stomach upsets, irritability and diarrhoea.

If you are drinking a lot of coffee, tea or cola and do decide to give it up, make sure you do so gradually - for example by reducing the number of cups per day gradually or substituting the odd drink for decaffeinated versions.

Stopping the intake of caffeine suddenly can lead to withdrawal symptoms including headaches, fatigue, moodiness and nausea.

SALT

Salt or sodium chloride - as it is chemically known- is both a food seasoning and a preservative. Cutting down on salt intake is not difficult to do.

Do we need to eat salt?

Yes, it is important for correct functioning of the body.

How much should we eat?

Recommendations are that we consume *no more than 2,500mg or 2.5g* each day (1/2 teaspoon). You must take into account the other sources of sodium other than the salt that you add to your plate such as processed foods, some drinks and snacks.

The **more processed a food is**, the *more likely it is* to contain **large amounts of salt.** These foods don't always taste salty but you can check their sodium content by looking at the list of ingredients on food labels.

Using highly salted foods **can cause** high blood pressure and hypertension (sustained high blood pressure).

The reason for this is that the salt gets dissolved into the bloodstream making the blood a **lot thicker** and unable to be utilised as efficiently by the cells. As a result of this the cells release water into the bloodstream, **raising the amount of blood** in the system which increases the workload placed on the heart. This causes an elevation in blood pressure. This excess water is then dealt with by the kidneys and urinated out of the body.

When a person loses fluid from the body- whether it is blood, sweat or urine- then the person **also loses electrolytes**. These electrolytes are crucial to the life-sustaining work of the body's vital organs.

If you suffer from high blood pressure **you should restrict salt intake** and increase your intake of potassium and calcium .

- Buy *fresh, natural foods* more often than processed foods.
- Use seasonings and spices **other than salt** to flavour foods
- Choose reduced sodium products wherever possible
- Always read food labels looking for the key words salt and sodium
- Leave the *salt shaker in the cupboard and not on the table*
- About 70% of our daily intake of salt is from **processed foods**
- Whole, unprocessed foods contribute to about 10% of salt in our diet
- Salt added to foods at the table or cooking amounts to 20% of our daily intake.

SHOPPING LISTS

1 - 5
WEEKS

WEEKS 1 AND 5 – **SHOPPING LIST**

Most foods are listed for specific meals but in some meals you will find just listed as 'fruit' or 'vegetables'. Due to personal choice and the seasonal nature of these foods you may need to substitute some and **buy extra for this reason.**

Vegetables can be fresh, or frozen. Fruit should be fresh, frozen or tinned in their own juice or apple juice, *not syrup.*

From week to week there may be foods you already have, simply select the ones you need. If you do choose foods of your own preference you will obviously have to take this into account.

VEGETABLES:

- 1lb carrots, celery, 2 peppers, frozen peas, 1 eggplant (aubergine), 2 zucchini (courgettes), 1 butternut squash,
- broccoli, 1 swede, 4 onions, 1 red onion, 2lb potatoes, baby potatoes, 1 garlic bulb, 3 red or
- green chillies

SALAD:

- cherry tomatoes, lettuce, cucumber, spring onions

FRUIT:

- 2 oranges, 3 bananas, 2 peaches, small punnet of strawberries, 1 apple, blueberries or 1
- small tin of pineapple chunks in natural juice

BREAKFAST CEREALS:

- Muesli (no added sugar or salt)
- Cornflakes
- Porridge oats

OTHER:

- Granulated sweetener
- 1 tin of kidney beans (no added salt or sugar)
- 1 tin of baked beans (no added sugar)
- 1 large punnet of mushrooms, 1 punnet of Porcini mushrooms
- Raisins
- Sunflower seeds
- Breadsticks
- 1 small tub of cottage cheese
- 1 tub of low-fat houmous
- 2 small tubs low-fat natural yoghurt
- 1 small wholemeal loaf
- 1 pack of wholemeal pittas
- 2 salmon fillets, 2 monkfish fillets, 2 tins of tuna
- 1 packet of Quorn or turkey mince
- 3 tins of chopped tomatoes
- Tomato puree
- 1 packet of rice cakes
- 1 packet of pasta
- 4 pints of half-fat milk
- 1 packet of wholegrain rice, 1 packet of risotto rice
- Olive oil, sunflower oil
- 1 treat food (moderation)
- 1 skinless chicken breast
- Paprika, mixed herbs, garam masala, black pepper, fresh chives, fresh parsley, black pepper
- Soy sauce
- Parmesan cheese
- Vegetable stock cubes or powder

2 - 6
WEEKS

WEEKS 2 AND 6 – **SHOPPING LIST**

Most foods are listed for specific meals but in some meals you will find just listed as 'fruit' or 'vegetables'. Due to personal choice and the seasonal nature of these foods you may need to substitute some and **buy extra for this reason.**

Vegetables can be fresh, or frozen. Fruit should be fresh, frozen or tinned in their own juice or apple juice, *not syrup*.

From week to week there may be foods you already have, simply select the ones you need. If you do choose foods of your own preference you will obviously have to take this into account.

VEGETABLES:

- ❍ 1lb carrots, celery, 2 red peppers, 2 yellow peppers, 1 green pepper, butternut squash,
- ❍ 4 onions, 2 red onions, 1 swede, broccoli, 2lbs potatoes, baby potatoes, 4 red or green
- ❍ chillies, 1 avocado, 4 large leeks, 1 garlic bulb, frozen peas

SALAD:

- ❍ cherry tomatoes, lettuce, cucumber, spring onions, 4 tomatoes,

FRUIT:

- ❍ 2 satsumas, 4 bananas, 2 peaches, 1 lime, 1 lemon, 2 punnets of fresh or frozen berries

BREAKFAST CEREALS:

- ❍ Muesli (no added sugar or salt)
- ❍ Cornflakes
- ❍ Porridge oats

OTHER:

- ❍ Granulated sweetener
- ❍ 2 eggs
- ❍ 2 tins baked beans
- ❍ 1 punnet of mushrooms
- ❍ 1 packet of sunflower seeds
- ❍ 1 packet of raw cashews
- ❍ 1 packet of raisins
- ❍ 1 small tub of cottage cheese
- ❍ 3 small tubs low-fat natural yoghurt
- ❍ 1 pack of wholemeal pittas, breadsticks, 1 packet of rice cakes, 1 small wholemeal loaf
- ❍ 3 tins of chopped tomatoes
- ❍ Tomato purée
- ❍ 1 packet of noodles
- ❍ 4 pints of half-fat milk
- ❍ 1 pack of Ryvita
- ❍ 1 packet of wholegrain rice
- ❍ Olive oil, sunflower oil, low-fat sunflower margarine
- ❍ 2 tins of kidney beans (no added salt or sugar)
- ❍ 1 tuna steak, 1 salmon steak, 1 white fish steak, mackerel, 1 packet of frozen prawns,
- ❍ 2 tins of tuna
- ❍ Quorn mince
- ❍ Black pepper
- ❍ Fresh parsley, oregano, mixed herbs, paprika, garam masala
- ❍ Tabasco sauce
- ❍ White sauce mix
- ❍ Yeast extract
- ❍ Vegetable stock cubes or powder
- ❍ 1 packet of make your own plain pop corn
- ❍ 1 treat food (moderation)

3 - 7
WEEKS

WEEKS 3 AND 7 – **SHOPPING LIST**

Most foods are listed for specific meals but in some meals you will find just listed as 'fruit' or 'vegetables'. Due to personal choice and the seasonal nature of these foods you may need to substitute some and **buy extra for this reason.**

Vegetables can be fresh, or frozen. Fruit should be fresh, frozen or tinned in their own juice or apple juice, *not syrup*.

From week to week there may be foods you already have, simply select the ones you need. If you do choose foods of your own preference you will obviously have to take this into account.

VEGETABLES:

- ❍ 4 carrots, celery, 1 red pepper, 1 green pepper, frozen peas, (eggplant) aubergine, courgettes, butternut squash, 4 onions, 1 red onion, swede, broccoli, potatoes, baby potatoes, 4 red chillies, baby corn, mangetout, 1 bulb of garlic, 1 punnet of mushrooms, frozen sweetcorn

SALAD:

- ❍ cherry tomatoes, lettuce, cucumber, spring onions, tomatoes

FRUIT:

- ❍ 1 orange, 2 bananas, 1 peach, small punnet of strawberries, 1 apple, 1 melon, blueberries or
- ❍ 1 small tin of pineapple chunks in juice

BREAKFAST CEREALS:

- Muesli (no added sugar or salt)
- Cornflakes
- Porridge oats

OTHER:

- Granulated sweetener
- 1 tin baked beans, 1 tin of kidney beans (no added salt or sugar)
- Packet of raisins
- Packet of sunflower seeds
- 2 small tubs of cottage cheese
- 1 tub of low-fat houmous
- 3 small tubs low-fat natural yoghurt
- 1 pack of wholemeal pittas, 1 small wholemeal loaf
- 1 salmon fillets
- 1 packet of Quorn or turkey mince, 1 Quorn roast
- 2 tins of chopped tomatoes
- Tomato purée
- 2 tins of tuna
- 1 packet of rice cakes
- 1 packet of pasta
- 4 pints of half-fat milk
- 1 pack of Ryvita
- 1 packet of wholegrain rice, 1 packet of noodles
- Olive oil, sunflower oil, low-fat sunflower margarine
- 1 treat food (moderation)
- 1 packet of make-your-own popcorn
- Peanut butter (no added sugar)
- Fresh ginger, fresh parsley
- Paprika, mixed herbs, garam masala, black pepper
- Light soy sauce
- 2 eggs
- Gravy granules
- Yeast extract
- Vegetable stock cubes or powder

4 - 8
WEEKS

WEEKS 4 AND 8 – **SHOPPING LIST**

Most foods are listed for specific meals but in some meals you will find just listed as 'fruit' or 'vegetables'. Due to personal choice and the seasonal nature of these foods you may need to substitute some and **buy extra for this reason.**

Vegetables can be fresh, or frozen. Fruit should be fresh, frozen or tinned in their own juice or apple juice, *not syrup*.

From week to week there may be foods you already have, simply select the ones you need. If you do choose foods of your own preference you will obviously have to take this into account.

VEGETABLES:

- ❍ 4 carrots, celery, 1 red pepper, 1 green pepper, frozen peas, frozen sweetcorn,
- ❍ 1 eggplant (aubergine), 1 zucchini (courgette), butternut squash, 4 onions, 1 red onion, broccoli, 2lb potatoes,
- ❍ baby potatoes, 4 leeks, 1 garlic bulb, 2 red or green chillies, 1 packet of baby corn, 1
- ❍ packet of mangetout

SALAD:

- ❍ cherry tomatoes, lettuce, cucumber, spring onions

FRUIT:

- ❍ 1 oranges, 4 bananas, small punnet of strawberries or frozen berries, 1 apple

BREAKFAST CEREALS:

- Muesli (no added sugar or salt)
- Cornflakes
- Porridge oats

OTHER:

- Granulated sweetener
- 4 pints half-fat milk
- 1 packet of raisins, 1 packet of sunflower seeds, 1 packet of pumpkin seeds
- 1 packet of make your own popcorn
- 2 small tubs of cottage cheese
- 1 small punnet of mushrooms
- 2 eggs
- 1 pack of Quorn sausages/low-fat sausages,1 pack of Quorn burgers
- 1 packet of Quorn or turkey mince
- 1 tin of baked beans
- 2 tins of tuna
- 1 tin of kidney beans (no added salt or sugar)
- Tabasco sauce, light soy sauce
- 2 small tubs low-fat natural yoghurt
- 2 tins of chopped tomatoes
- Tomato purée
- 1 small wholemeal loaf, breadsticks, 1 packet of rice cakes
- 1 packet of pasta
- 1 pack of Ryvita
- 2 salmon steaks, 1 white fish steak, mackerel
- Olive oil, sunflower oil, low-fat sunflower margarine
- Taco shells
- Yeast extract
- Fresh chopped parsley, fresh ginger, black pepper, basil
- 1 packet of noodles
- 1 treat food (moderation)
- Vegetable stock cubes or powder
- White sauce mix
- Low-fat cheese

DAILY MENUS

1-5 WEEKS

WEEKS 1 AND 5 – **MENUS**

All meal times are approximate. **The key thing is to eat regularly.** Drink a minimum of 2 litres of water regularly throughout the day.

	7.30am Breakfast	10.30am Snack	1.00pm Lunch	4.30pm Snack	7.30pm Dinner
Monday	Porridge with Sweetener + Half-Fat Milk	Raisins + Sunflower Seeds	Wholemeal Pitta, Salmon + Cherry Tomato	1 Orange	Quorn Chilli + Wholegrain Rice
Tuesday	Sugar-Free Muesli + Half-Fat Milk	Vegetable Sticks + Houmous	Quorn Chilli Salad	Low-Fat Natural Yoghurt + Fruit	Mushroom Risotto
Wednesday	Porridge with Sweetener + Half-Fat Milk	Banana Glass of Half-Fat Milk	Tuna Salad	Raisins + Sunflower Seeds	Baked Potato Cottage Cheese + Cherry Tomato
Thursday	Sugar-Free Muesli + Half-Fat Milk	Breadsticks	Vegetable Soup + Rice Cakes	Fruit Smoothie	Poached Salmon, Potato Wedges + Broccoli

	7.30am Breakfast	10.30am Snack	1.00pm Lunch	4.30pm Snack	7.30pm Dinner
Friday	Cornflakes + Half-fat Milk	Cold Baby Potatoes	Baked Beans + Wholemeal Toast	2 Rice Cakes with Cottage Cheese + Cherry Tomato	Tuna Pasta Bake
Saturday	Porridge with Sweetener + Half-fat Milk	1 Banana + 1 Peach	Chicken Salad	Baby New Potatoes	Take Away or Meal Out of Your Choice
Sunday	Sugar-Free Muesli + Half-Fat Milk	Vegetable Sticks + Houmous	Fruit Salad + Low-fat Yoghurt	Treat Food OF Your Choice	Monkfish + Roasted Vegetables + Tomato Sauce

2 - 6
WEEKS

WEEKS 2 AND 6 – **MENUS**

All meal times are approximate. **The key thing is to eat regularly.** Drink a minimum of 2 litres of water regularly throughout the day.

	7.30am Breakfast	10.30am Snack	1.00pm Lunch	4.30pm Snack	7.30pm Dinner
Monday	Porridge with Sweetener + Half-Fat Milk	Raisins + Sunflower Seeds	Prawn and Avocado Salad	Banana Glass of Semi-Skimmed Milk	Leek and Potato Soup
Tuesday	Sugar-Free Muesli + Half-Fat Milk	Plain Popcorn	Leek and Potato Soup 1 Slice Wholemeal Toast	Low-Fat Natural Yoghurt + Fruit	Fish Pie + Broccoli
Wednesday	Porridge with Sweetener + Half-Fat Milk	2 Satsumas	Mackerel Salad	Raisins + Raw Cashews	Baked Potato + Baked Beans
Thursday	Sugar-Free Muesli + Half-Fat Milk	Banana and a Glass of Semi-Skimmed Milk	Vegetable Sticks + Tomato Salsa	Fruit Smoothie	Bean Goulash with Noodles

Friday	Cornflakes + Half-Fat Milk	Cold Baby Potatoes	Baked Beans + Wholemeal Toast	1 Ryvita with Cottage Cheese + Cherry Tomato	Take Away or Meal Out of Your Choice
Saturday	Scrambled Egg 1 Slice W/ Meal Toast + Grilled Tomatoes	Fruit Smoothie	Vegetable Soup + Rice Cakes	Vegetable Sticks + Tomato Salsa	Tuna, Roasted Vegetables + Tomato Sauce
Sunday	Sugar-Free Muesli + Half-Fat Milk	Vegetable Sticks	Chicken Salad	Treat Food OF Your Choice	Vegetable Chilli + Wholegrain Rice

3 - 7
WEEKS

WEEKS 3 AND 7 – **MENUS**

All meal times are approximate. **The key thing is to eat regularly.** Drink a minimum of 2 litres of water regularly throughout the day.

	7.30am Breakfast	10.30am Snack	1.00pm Lunch	4.30pm Snack	7.30pm Dinner
Monday	Sugar-free Muesli + Semi-Skimmed Milk	Vegetable Sticks + Houmous	Baked Potato Cottage Cheese + Baked Beans	Raisins + Sunflower Seeds	Pasta and Tomato Sauce with Vegetables
Tuesday	Porridge with Sweetener + Semi-Skimmed Milk	Low-fat Natural Yoghurt + Fruit	Tuna Salad Sandwich	Banana Glass of Semi-skimmed Milk	Salmon + Vegetable Stir Fry with Noodles
Wednesday	Sugar-free Muesli + Semi-Skimmed Milk	2 Slices of Melon Glass of Milk	Rice Cakes with Cottage Cheese + Cherry Tomato	Fruit Smoothie	Quorn Chilli + Wholegrain Rice
Thursday	Sugar-free Muesli + Half-fat Milk	Small Bowl of Plain Popcorn	Baked Potato Cottage Cheese + Tuna	6 Strawberries 1 Peach	Butternut Squash Soup + Rice Cakes

	7.30am Breakfast	10.30am Snack	1.00pm Lunch	4.30pm Snack	7.30pm Dinner
Friday	Cornflakes + Semi-skimmed Milk	1 Ryvita with Cottage Cheese	Butternut Squash Soup	Apple	Moussaka, Broccoli and New Potatoes
Saturday	Scrambled Egg 1 Slice W/ Meal Toast + Grilled Tomatoes	1 Orange	1 Pitta Bread with Quorn + Roasted Vegetables	Vegetable Sticks + Houmous	Take Away or Meal Out of Your Choice
Sunday	Sugar-free Muesli + Semi-skimmed Milk	Vegetable Sticks	Rice Cakes with Peanut Butter (no added sugar) or Soft Cheese	Treat Food of Your Choice	Quorn Roast + Vegetables, Mashed Potato + Gravy

4 - 8
WEEKS

WEEKS 4 AND 8 – **MENUS**

All meal times are approximate. **The key thing is to eat regularly.** Drink a minimum of 2 litres of water regularly throughout the day.

	7.30am Breakfast	10.30am Snack	1.00pm Lunch	4.30pm Snack	7.30pm Dinner
Monday	Porridge with Sweetener + Semi-skimmed Milk	Raisins + Sunflower Seeds	Baked Potato Cottage Cheese	1 Apple	Quorn Burgers, Salad + Potato Wedges
Tuesday	Porridge with Sweetener + Semi-skimmed Milk	2 Sticks of Celery	Poached Eggs, Baked Beans + Quorn Sausage	Raisins + Pumpkin Seeds	Fish Pie + Vegetables
Wednesday	Sugar-free Muesli + Semi-skimmed Milk	Strawber-ries	Tuna Salad Sandwich	Banana Glass of Semi-skimmed Milk	Bean Tacos + Wholegrain Rice
Thursday	Porridge with Sweetener + Semi-skimmed Milk	1 Banana + Glass of Milk	Rice Cakes with Cottage Cheese + Cherry Tomato	Fruit Smoothie	Vegetable Moussaka, New Potatoes + Salad

	7.30am Breakfast	10.30am Snack	1.00pm Lunch	4.30pm Snack	7.30pm Dinner
Friday	Cornflakes + Semi-skimmed Milk	Cold Baby Potatoes	Mackerel Salad	1 Ryvita with Cottage Cheese + Cherry Tomato	Salmon + Vegetable Stir Fry and Noodles
Saturday	Porridge with Sweetener + Semi-skimmed Milk	Breadsticks	Fruit Salad + Low-fat Yoghurt	Vegetable Sticks	Take Away or Meal Out of Your Choice
Sunday	Sugar-free Muesli + Semi-skimmed Milk	Plain Popcorn	Leek and Potato Soup	Treat Food of Your Choice	Tuna Pasta Bake and Salad

RECIPES

POACHED SALMON, POTATO WEDGES AND BROCCOLI (serves 1)

- 1 salmon fillet
- 1 large potato
- 50g/ 2oz broccoli, cut into florets
- 2 tsp olive oil
- Salt and freshly milled black pepper
- 1 tsp paprika
- 1/2 tsp hot chilli powder

Potato Wedges

1. Scrub the potato and chop into large wedges.
2. Put the prepared potato, olive oil, paprika, chilli powder, salt and pepper in a mixing bowl and stir until all the ingredients are evenly combined and wedges are coated.
3. Cook in a pre heated oven at 200 °c, gas mark 6 for 40-50 minutes.

Poached Salmon

1. Bring a pan of water to simmering point.
2. Add salmon making sure it is completely covered with water.
3. Bring back to simmering point and cook for 4-5mins.

Broccoli

- Steam or boil broccoli for 10-15mins or until tender.

SALMON STIR FRY (serves 2)

- 2 salmon fillets
- 6 baby corn
- 25g mange tout
- ½ red pepper
- 4 chopped spring onions
- 1 carrot, finely sliced
- Noodles (allow 1 strip per person)
- ½ tbsp olive oil

For the sauce:

- 1 tsp fresh ginger, finely chopped
- 2 red chillies, finely chopped
- 1 clove of garlic, finely chopped
- 1 tbsp light soy sauce

PREPARATION

1. Prepare the sauce first by placing all the ingredients in a bowl together, stirring to combine evenly and then set aside.
2. Heat oil in a suitable pan and add corn, mange tout, pepper, carrots and spring onions. Cook for 5 minutes on a medium heat.
3. Meanwhile add noodles to a pan of boiling water and cook as per instructions.
4. Add salmon and cook until colour changes.
5. Finally add sauce and cook for a further minute.

MUSHROOM RISOTTO
(serves 2)

- 15g/½ oz dried Porcini mushrooms
- 50g/2oz fresh mushrooms, finely chopped
- 100g/4oz risotto rice
- 1 tsp olive oil
- ½ red onion, finely chopped
- ½ garlic clove, chopped small
- 300ml/½ pint vegetable stock
- 1 dsp grated Parmesan cheese
- 1 dsp finely chopped fresh parsley

PREPARATION

1. Soak the porcini mushrooms in a small bowl of warm water for about 30 minutes, then drain and chop finely.
2. Heat the oil in a saucepan and fry the onion and garlic for 5 minutes. In a separate saucepan heat the stock.
3. Add the porcini mushrooms to the onions, if they stick add a little water. Cook for 2 minutes then add the rice, stir for a further 3 minutes and then add a little stock.
4. Stirring constantly add a ladle of stock. When this one has been absorbed add another. Continue until all the stock is used in this way, and then add the mushrooms.
5. Continue to cook until the mushrooms are cooked and the rice is al dente, the risotto should be moist.
6. Remove from heat, stir in parmesan and parsley and serve immediately.
7. Serve with a salad.

CHILLI BEAN TACOS
(serves 2)

- ½ red pepper, ½ green pepper, both diced
- 25g/1oz sweetcorn
- 1 small red onion finely chopped
- 400g tin drained kidney beans (no sugar/salt added) in water (juice reserved)
- ½ tsp Tabasco sauce
- 2 garlic cloves crushed
- 2 tbsp tomato puree
- 4 taco shells

For garnish:

- Lettuce
- Onion
- 25g low-fat cheese grated

PREPARATION

1. Place the peppers, sweetcorn and onion in a saucepan and cover with a small amount of boiling water and simmer for 10 minutes.
2. Add the kidney beans, Tabasco sauce, garlic and tomato puree and enough of the reserved juice to make a thick sauce, simmer for another 10 minutes.
3. Heat taco shells according to packet instructions.
4. Fill taco shells with vegetable mixture and top with lettuce, onion and a small amount of cheese.
5. Serve with salad, wholemeal rice or couscous.

VEGETABLE MOUSSAKA (serves 2-3)

- 1 medium sized onion, finely chopped
- 1 garlic clove, crushed and finely chopped
- 25g/1oz mushrooms diced
- 1 large aubergine
- 3 tomatoes
- 50g Quorn mince
- 1 tbsp tomato puree
- 1 tsp yeast extract
- 1 tbsp fresh finely chopped parsley
- ¼ pint of vegetable stock
- olive oil
- salt and freshly ground black pepper

For the topping:

- ¼ pint low-fat natural yoghurt
- 2 eggs
- Salt and pepper

PREPARATION

1. Slice the aubergine in half lengthways. Place on a baking tray, drizzle with olive oil and bake in the oven at 180c, gas mark 4 for 30 – 40 minutes or until tender.
2. Heat a teaspoon of the oil in a non stick saucepan and sauté the onion and garlic on a low heat until the onions are transparent.
3. Add Quorn or turkey mince, mushrooms, tomatoes, tomato puree, vegetable stock, yeast extract and fresh parsley, cover

and simmer over a low heat for approximately 30 minutes or until a thick consistency is reached and mince is cooked. Season to taste.

4. When aubergine is cooked, allow to cool slightly and then slice thinly.
5. Layer the aubergine and sauce finishing with a layer of aubergine.
6. For the topping whisk the eggs and yoghurt together, season and pour over the moussaka.
7. Cook in a pre-heated oven at 180c, gas mark 4 for 35 – 45 minutes or until topping is golden brown.
8. Serve with a salad.

TOMATO SAUCE

- 1 red onion
- 400g tin chopped tomatoes
- 1 tbsp tomato puree
- 2 tsp paprika (optional)
- 1 tsp oregano or basil
- 1 tbsp olive oil

PREPARATION

1. Finely chop red onion and sauté until transparent.
2. Add paprika if using this adds heat if liked and cook for a further minute stirring continuously.
3. Add remaining ingredients and season with salt and pepper.
4. Cover and simmer on a low heat for 20 – 30 minutes until sauce thickens.

BEAN GOULASH
(serves 2)

- 1 red pepper, ½ yellow and ½ green pepper
- 1 medium sized onion
- 400g tin drained kidney beans (no sugar/salt added)
- Cup of mushrooms
- 300ml/ ¾ pint vegetable stock
- 1 tbsp tomato puree
- 1 tsp mixed herbs
- 3 tsp paprika
- 1 clove of garlic
- Freshly ground black pepper
- 2 tsp olive oil

PREPARATION

1. Finely chop onion and garlic, dice peppers and slice mushrooms.
2. Heat oil in saucepan and sauté onion and garlic until onions are transparent.
3. Add paprika and cook for 1 minute, stirring continuously.
4. Add mushrooms and peppers and cook for a further minute, continue stirring.
5. Add remaining ingredients and simmer uncovered until peppers become tender and sauce thickens.
6. Serve with brown rice, couscous or noodles.

Diced chicken can be added to this if preferred.

TUNA PASTA BAKE (serves 3-4)

- 1 medium onion
- 1 cup of mushrooms
- 1 drained tin of tuna in spring water or brine
- 400g tin chopped tomatoes
- 300ml/½ pint vegetable stock
- 100g whole wheat pasta
- 1 tbsp tomato puree
- 1 clove garlic crushed
- 2 tsp olive oil
- 1 tbsp chopped fresh basil or 1 tsp dried basil
- Freshly ground black pepper
- 25g/1 oz grated low-fat cheese
- 1 sliced tomato

PREPARATION

1. Finely chop onions and garlic and sauté in heated oil until transparent.
2. Slice mushrooms, add to onions and garlic and cook for a further 2 minutes stirring all the time.
3. Add chopped tomatoes, tomato puree, chopped basil, vegetable stock and season with black pepper.
4. Lower heat and simmer for 20 minutes or until sauce thickens.
5. Add tuna and cook for a further 2 minutes.
6. Cook pasta as per packet instructions.
7. Add cooked pasta, stir in well and transfer mixture into an oven proof dish.
8. Sprinkle with a little cheese and cook uncovered in a pre heated oven at 200 °c, gas mark 6 for 20 – 30 minutes until cheese is melted and golden brown.
9. Serve with a salad.

CHILLI AND RICE
(serves 2-3)

- 1lb lean turkey mince or ½ packet of Quorn mince
- 1 medium onion
- 1 red pepper
- 400g tin drained kidney beans (no sugar/salt added) in water
- 1-2 red chillies, seeds removed, finely chopped
- 400g tin chopped tomatoes
- 1 tbsp tomato puree
- 1-2 cloves garlic, finely chopped
- 2 tsp paprika
- 1 tsp mixed herbs
- 2 tsp olive oil

For the rice:

- 1 cup of wholegrain rice, washed in 2 changes of water
- 1 medium onion
- 2 cups vegetable stock
- 2 tsp olive oil
- 1 tsp garam masala
- 2 tsp soy sauce

PREPARATION

1. Finely chop onion, pepper, chillies and garlic and sauté in oil over a low heat for 5 minutes.
2. Add mince and stir regularly.
3. Add paprika and cook for a further minute, stirring constantly.

4. Add tomatoes, herbs and season with salt and pepper and cook for 30 minutes or until mince is thoroughly cooked and peppers soft.
5. Add a little water or vegetable stock during cooking if required.

For the rice:

1. Finely chop onions and sauté in oil until transparent.
2. Add rice and cook on a low heat covered for a further 3 minutes.
3. Add vegetable stock, garam masala and soy sauce and simmer gently covered for 30 minutes or until rice is tender and water is absorbed.
4. Add more water during cooking if required.

SMALL FRUIT SMOOTHIE
(serves 2)

- 1 banana, cut into chunks
- 4 strawberries
- 1 tbsp blueberries
- 6 raspberries
- 150ml/¼ pint natural low-fat yoghurt
- 2 tsp granulated sweetener if required
- A few ice cubes

PREPARATION

1. Place all the ingredients in a blender and blend until smooth.
2. Pour into a glass and serve immediately.

TUNA, ROASTED VEGETABLES AND TOMATO SAUCE (serves 1)

- Fresh tuna steak
- 1 potato
- ½ butternut squash
- ½ red pepper
- 1 small courgette
- 1 red onion
- ½ tbsp olive oil

For the tomato sauce:

- 1 red onion
- 400g tin chopped tomatoes
- 1 tbsp tomato puree
- 2 tsp paprika (optional)
- 1 tsp oregano or basil
- 1 tbsp olive oil

PREPARATION

1. Scrub potato and cut into wedges. Peel butternut squash and cut into 1 inch chunks. Chop pepper into 1 inch chunks, thickly slice courgette and chop red onion into large chunks. Place in a large mixing bowl, add oil, salt and pepper and mix together thoroughly until all evenly coated.
2. Place on a baking sheet and cook in the oven at 200 °c or gas mark 6 for 35 – 45 minutes until all vegetables are tender.

For the sauce:

1. Finely chop red onion and sauté until transparent.
2. Add paprika if desired, and cook for a further minute stirring continuously.
3. Add remaining ingredients and season with salt and pepper.
4. Cover and simmer on a low heat for 20 – 30 minutes until sauce thickens.

Cook the tuna on either a non stick frying pan or griddle pan until cooked through, or to desired taste.

BUTTERNUT SQUASH AND SWEETCORN SOUP (serves 3)

- 1 medium butternut squash chopped into 1 inch cubes
- 100g / 4 oz frozen sweetcorn
- ½ tbsp sunflower oil
- 1 medium onion peeled and finely chopped
- 8 fl oz semi-skimmed milk
- 1 pint / 600ml hot vegetable stock made with Marigold Swiss vegetable bouillon powder
- Salt and freshly milled black pepper

PREPARATION

1. Heat the oil in large saucepan, then add the onion and soften for about 5 minutes.
2. Add the butternut squash and sweetcorn, stir and season to taste with salt and pepper. Cover and sweat on a low heat for 10 minutes.
3. Pour in the milk and stock and simmer gently for a further 20 minutes.
4. Allow to cool slightly and then blend to a puree leaving a little texture.
5. Serve with toasted wholemeal pittas or warm wholemeal bread.

LEEK, ONION AND POTATO SOUP (serves 3)

- 4 large leeks
- 1 medium onion, peeled and finely chopped
- 2 medium potatoes peeled and diced
- ½ tbsp sunflower oil
- 1 ½ pints/850 mls hot vegetable stock
- 10fl oz/275 ml semi-skimmed milk
- Salt and freshly milled black pepper
- To serve – 1½ tbsp snipped fresh chives or parsley

PREPARATION

1. Begin by trimming the leeks, discarding the tough outer layer, now split them in half lengthways and slice them finely. Wash thoroughly in 2 or 3 changes of clean water and drain well.
2. Heat the oil in large saucepan, then add the onion, leeks and potato, stir them around, season with salt and pepper then cover and allow to sweat over a very low heat for about 15 minutes.
3. Pour in the milk and stock, cover and simmer gently for a further 20 minutes.
4. Allow to cool slightly and then blend to a puree.
5. Return to the pan, reheat and stir in the snipped chives or chopped parsley.
6. Serve with a toasted wholemeal pitta or warm wholemeal bread.

VEGETABLE SOUP
(serves 3)

- 1 carrot peeled and diced
- 1 swede peeled and diced
- 1 potato peeled and diced
- 3 tbsp frozen peas
- You can substitute any of the above for your own choice of vegetables
- ½ tbsp sunflower oil
- 1 medium onion peeled and finely chopped
- 1 pint / 600ml hot vegetable stock
- Salt and freshly milled black pepper
- Yeast extract
- 1 tbsp chopped fresh parsley
- 2 tsp cornflower (blended with a little cold water)

PREPARATION

1. Heat the oil in a large saucepan, then add the onion and soften for about 5 minutes.
2. Add the remaining vegetables and yeast extract, stir and season to taste with salt and pepper. Cover and sweat on a low heat for 10 minutes.
3. Pour in the stock and simmer gently for a further 20 minutes.
4. Stir in the cornflower and cook for a further minute. Season to taste and serve.

Spicy Tomato Salsa

- 75g/3oz tomato, finely chopped
- 25g/1oz onion, peeled and finely chopped
- 1tsp finely chopped fresh or dried oregano
- ½ tsp ground cumin
- 1 dsp freshly squeezed lemon juice
- 1 tsp freshly squeezed lime juice
- 4 drops Tabasco sauce
- ½ tsp chopped garlic

PREPARATION

1. Make the salsa by placing all the ingredients in a bowl and stirring well.
2. Can be served with fish, meat and vegetables to make a tasty accompaniment.

FISH PIE
(serves 2)

- 4 medium sized potatoes
- 3 spring onions, finely chopped
- Salmon
- Haddock or other white fish
- White sauce mix (packet)
- 2 tbsp milk
- 2 tsp low-fat margarine
- Freshly ground black pepper
- 2 tsp olive oil

PREPARATION

1. Peel and chop potato then boil until cooked.
2. Drain and then mash potatoes with milk and margarine.
3. Add chopped spring onions, black pepper and season to taste.
4. Prepare white sauce as directed or prepare your own.
5. Poach fish until just cooked, drain and place in a casserole dish.
6. Add white sauce to fish so all fish is coated.
7. Add mashed potato and cook in a pre heated oven 200°c, gas mark 6 for 20 minutes.
8. Serve with vegetables of your choice.

10

CHAPTER

FLEXIBILITY AND STRETCHING **FOR RUNNERS**

The more you exercise and run, the more prone you become to muscular imbalances. The lower back, calves, and hamstrings can become tight and inflexible while the shins, quadriceps, and stomach muscles may actually get weaker in comparison. Stretching will help to counteract this.

Flexibility is one the most often overlooked parts of health and fitness. Flexibility naturally diminishes with age, but also as you start to increase your distances you will notice that your muscles seem to be getting a little tighter.

Runners need to primarily concentrate on stretching off the muscles of the legs and lower back in order to return them to their pre-exercise length.

Always warm the muscles up first before stretching by walking briskly or gentle jogging for 5 minutes. This helps to increase heat in the area, making the muscles more pliable and less likely to tear if stretched too vigorously. This means if you want to stretch before exercise, you should do so after an initial warm up period.

Stretching before exercise is not necessary, but it certainly won't hurt if you choose to. The important time to stretch is after exercise. During exercise the muscles contract repeatedly, leading to slightly shorter and tighter muscles, which need help to be lengthened and stretched out. This is where stretching is very beneficial as it returns the muscles to their pre-exercise state.

Regular stretching offers the following benefits:

- Helps prevent muscular aches, pains, and cramping

- Reduces the possibility of muscular soreness over the following days
- Decreases the possibility of suffering mechanical muscular injuries
- Increases the muscles' ability to lengthen and stretch during exercise
- Improves the muscles' ability to work faster, harder, and more efficiently
- Allows you to safely improve stride length
- Improves overall posture and running technique

You should use static stretching instead of ballistic stretching to safely lengthen your muscles and improve flexibility.

BALLISTIC STRETCHING

Ballistic stretching is a very advanced form of stretching used to aggressively improve the muscles' ability to lengthen. It is not advisable to attempt this unsupervised and without sufficient experience or physiological knowledge.

During ballistic stretching, you bounce into the stretch in an attempt to beat the stretch reflex (the sensation or sharp pain you receive that stops you from going too far when trying to increase the length or duration of a stretch).

STATIC STRETCHING

Static stretching involves taking the muscle to the point of its greatest range of motion, without overextending it. Done correctly, you should get a slight feeling of tightness or mild discomfort at about 6 or 7 on the RPE scale. This should not be a sharp or shooting pain; that would indicate that you are stretching too far and should ease back a little. This sharp pain is called the stretch reflex and its job is to ensure that you don't take the muscles further into a stretch than they are comfortably able to go. The way we improve flexibility is by working with the stretch reflex which is known as developmental stretching. You can do this as follows:

- Get into a stretch position and take the muscle to a point where you can feel a mild discomfort - just a little further back from where you felt a sharper pain (the stretch reflex).
- Wait for approximately 15 – 20 seconds without pushing any further until the discomfort becomes milder and then ease slowly further into the stretch until you again feel the stretch reflex. Ease back a little from here and hold this position.
- This can be repeated a few times, but ideally you should move onto another muscle after a minute to avoid stressing the muscle too far.

When stretching after running you need to focus on all the main muscles groups you've used in your session. These are:

- Quadriceps – the muscles that run down the front of your thighs, crossing the knee and hip joints
- Hamstrings – the muscles down the back of the legs
- Adductors – the muscles on the inside of the thighs at the top of the legs
- Hip Flexors – the muscles at the top and front of the thighs
- Gluteus Maximus – the muscles of the buttocks
- Gastrocnemius – the longest muscle in the calves just below the knee
- Soleus – the shorter muscle of the calves just above the ankle

The following advice should be adhered to when stretching:

- Do not overextend the muscles.
- You should feel very minimal tightness/ discomfort (but not pain).
- Hold and control the stretch for at least 15 - 30 seconds.

- Stretch all the major leg muscle groups as listed above.
- Stretch uniformly (after stretching one leg, stretch the other).
- Don't overstretch an injured area as this may cause additional damage.
- Never bounce when stretching as this can increase your chances of suffering an injury!

Always include stretching after a run; make it part of the training and cool down process, get into the habit. Your legs will be the most receptive to the benefits of stretching straight after you run. Stretch gently and slowly and while your muscles are still warm.

If your flexibility is quite poor, a regular program of stretching will help to rectify the problem. Stretching every day is a good idea, but always after you have warmed the muscles up first.

ROADSIDE **STRETCHES**

GASTROCNEMIUS (UPPER CALF) STRETCH

- Stand tall with one leg in front of the other, hands flat and at shoulder height against a wall
- Keep your hips facing the wall with the rear leg and spine in a straight line and bend your front leg
- Push against the wall and press the back heel into the ground, there shouldn't be any pressure on the front foot
- You should feel the stretch in the calf of the straight leg
- Repeat with the other leg

SOLEUS (LOWER CALF) STRETCH

- Standing as above, bring your back foot in closer to the wall and bend the bent leg a little further
- Keep both feet flat on the floor- you should feel a stretch in your lower calf of the back leg
- Leaning towards the wall intensifies the stretch
- There should be little pressure on the front foot
- Repeat with the other leg

STANDING QUADRICEPS (FRONT OF THIGH) STRETCH

- Lean against a wall and bend your right knee, grasping the right foot with your right hand behind you
- Lift your foot backwards until your heel is as close as possible to the buttocks, without touching
- Flex your foot and keep your body straight
- Push the hips a little further forward if you can't feel the stretch down the front of the thighs
- Repeat with the other leg

HAMSTRING (BACK OF THIGH) STRETCH

- Stand with your left foot placed flat on the ground in front of you and keep your extended leg straight
- Bend the right thigh, stick your bottom out and place your hands on your bent leg for support
- Lean forwards into your straight leg, pushing your bottom out, then straighten your upper body until you can feel a stretch down the back of the straight leg
- Repeat with the other leg

HIP FLEXOR (FRONT OF UPPER THIGH) STRETCH

- Take a long lunge forward
- Keep your hips square and your upper body vertical
- Place your hands on your front thigh
- Dip your back knee towards the ground until you feel a stretch down the back thigh, high up towards the top of your leg
- Repeat with the other leg

ADDUCTOR (INNER THIGH) STRETCH

- Stand tall with both feet pointing forwards, approximately two shoulders width apart
- Bend the right leg, place both hands on the bent thigh and lower the body towards the ground, keeping the left leg straight
- Keep your back straight and chest out
- You should feel this stretch high up the leg on the inside just below the groin of the straight leg
- Repeat with the other leg

STANDING GLUTE (BUTTOCKS) STRETCH

- Lean with your back against a wall for support
- Take hold of your right leg with both arms around the calf
- Pull in towards the chest until you can feel a stretch down the back of the right buttock
- Repeat with the other leg

STANDING TIBIALIS STRETCH

- Stand with your feet a hips width apart and your knees slightly bent
- Bend your right knee and grasp the toes of your right foot with your right hand, move your right knee forward
- Pull up on your toes forcing the top of your foot towards the ground
- You should feel this stretch down the front of the right shin
- Place one hand against a wall for balance if necessary
- Repeat with the other leg

COMBINED **STRETCHES**

The stretching techniques below allow you to stretch a number of muscles at the same time, which means you can stretch much quicker. These can be done at home where you can use either a mat or towel to sit on.

LYING QUADRICEPS AND TIBIALIS STRETCH

- Sit down on to the floor on your bent knees with your buttocks on top of your feet
- Make sure the tops of your feet are flat on the floor with your toes pointing towards your back
- Gently lean backwards as far as you can comfortably go until you can feel the stretch down the front of the thighs and the shins

HAMSTRING AND ADDUCTOR STRETCH

- Sit on the ground with both legs straight out in front of you
- Bend the left leg and place the sole of the left foot alongside the knee of the right leg
- Allow the right leg to lie relaxed on the ground and bend forward, keeping the back straight
- You should feel the stretch down the back of the left leg and inside of the right upper thigh
- Repeat with the other leg

SIMULTANEOUS GASTROCNEMIUS STRETCH

- Using a wall for support, place both hands against it and take a wide stride backwards
- Keep both heels flat on the floor
- Lean forwards keeping your back and legs straight
- You should feel this stretch in both calves at the same time

GLUTEUS AND LOWER BACK STRETCH

- Lying on the floor on your back
- Wrap both arms around the front of the shins and pull the thighs in towards the body
- Round your spine and hold that position
- You should be feeling this stretch on the lower back and around the buttocks

FINAL THOUGHTS

- Don't stretch cold muscles. It is far better to stretch after a run than before one.
- Do stretch lightly before doing any speed training – and always after a 5–10 minute warm up.
- Ease into your stretches gently, don't bounce or force them.
- After a run, hold each stretch for 30 seconds and repeat once or twice on each leg.

11 CHAPTER ALL ABOUT **INJURIES**

Perhaps the biggest challenge to any beginner starting a running program is not completing the actual race but making it to race day without any serious or niggling injuries.

Unfortunately, the truth is that most runners will pick up an injury of some sort at one time or another at times during their training. The causes of these injuries can be wide and varied, but almost all involve the lower body and many of them can be avoided if the correct technique, training plan, and running shoes have been chosen.

The way you run can dictate your chances of suffering from injuries because most running injuries are caused by muscle tightness, weakness, or imbalances. These also make your running form less efficient and more stressful on the joints.

Usually, the landing part of your stride is the cause of injuries you may suffer from because of the impact transmitted throughout the body with each step. This can be so great that any slight flaws in your running style are magnified enormously.

Injuries can be classified into 2 main groups: acute or chronic. Acute running injuries can usually be identified the moment they have been caused. For example, a bone may break during a fall or a muscle may tear while training. Treatment of this type of injury usually requires rest, meaning you will not be aggravating the damaged area and therefore recovery can be quite rapid.

Chronic injuries develop over time and can be difficult to heal. Because they are not as severe in nature, many runners continue through them, even though their training may have to be reduced slightly. This can often lead to quite serious long-term problems.

COMMON RUNNING INJURIES

Shin Splints

This is a generic term for pain at the front of the shins. It actually encompasses a range of different problems that can occur around the shin bone itself, from muscle tightness, nerve pain to stress. A change in running technique, frequency, or running surface are all known triggers.

Muscle Tears

Muscle tears aren't a common injury that runners suffer because they don't need to make sudden explosive or quick twisting movements.

Ligament Tears

Ligament tears can be a problem with runners - especially in the ankles or knees, and are usually caused by a misplaced foot.

Ilio-Tibial Band Syndrome (ITB syndrome)

The ilio-tibial band is a muscle down the outside of the leg. When this becomes larger through constant use, it can rub against a piece of bone/fatpad just above the knee. There are several factors which could bring on this type of knee pain including muscular imbalance, weakness, poor leg alignment, and a change in running style.

Achilles Tendonitis

This is perhaps the most common injury suffered by runners and accounts for over 20% of all running injuries. The Achilles tendon is located at the back of the heel. Pain in this area can have a number of sources. Fatigue in the calf muscle, change in running technique, nerve damage, and poor circulation are all known triggers.

Plantar Fasciitis

This is a pain in the middle of the sole of foot and is caused by an abnormal landing foot position or calf muscles that are too tight. Choosing the right footwear can make a huge difference to ease this problem.

Piriformis Syndrome

The piriformis is a deep muscle of the buttocks. This muscle stabilises the body during training. The muscle can go into spasm or become inflamed. When it does this, because of its close proximity to the sciatic nerve, it can press against the nerve, causing pain down the leg and in the buttocks. Stretching the muscle is usually considered to be the best preventative treatment.

Stress Fracture

The most common acute injury experienced while training for a marathon is a stress fracture. A stress fracture is an incomplete fracture of a bone caused by repeated stress (for example, the constant pounding of the foot on a pavement). Rest is the only option for the complete healing of a stress fracture.

Patello-femoral joint pain (PFJP)

Patello-femoral joint pain is one of the top five problems runners can suffer from. The reason for this is that the patella bone (kneecap) and surrounding tissues can cause the problem. The shape or position of the patella may be abnormal or there may be damage to the surrounding tissues. Running gait and landing foot position are both common causes of PFJP. Changes in frequency, duration, or intensity of training are the most common triggers for this complaint.

Foot pain

Foot pain is a very common runner's complaint which can be caused by stress fractures, plantar fasciitis, and blisters. Treatment depends on the problem, but once again, look for and then treat that trigger to ensure that this doesn't happen again.

Runner's Knee

This is the wearing away of the back of the kneecap during training for a 5k, and it causes strong pain in the knee. It primarily occurs because of an imbalance between the hamstrings and quadriceps muscles or wearing running shoes that do not give the right type of support.

Be cautious throughout your training. Some of these injuries can end your training for a long time.

LESS SERIOUS INJURIES

Blisters

Many people suffer from blisters needlessly; they are a constant threat to runners, but they can be avoided. By selecting specialist running socks, applying petroleum jelly to the feet prior to running, and wearing in new trainers gradually, you should be able to avoid this runner's blight.

Damage to the toenails

The constant impact and movement of your feet sliding to the front of your trainers is the usual cause of this complaint. To avoid this make sure that your trainers are a really good fit. (See section on selecting the correct footwear.)

Runner's nipple

This problem manifests itself by the constant friction of clothing over the nipple area. This repeated rubbing can cause inflammation and bleeding of the nipple. To avoid this, either cover the nipples in a layer of petroleum jelly or cover the nipple with a sticking plaster.

Apply Body Glide, Skin Lube, Lanacane, Vaseline or similar products (on feet, under arms, between thighs, on and around nipples, etc.) to eliminate the chances of suffering from chafing and blisters.

Cramp

Muscle cramping is when a muscle begins to spasm and contract intensely. The exact causes of muscle cramps are often debated, but the most likely reasons are dehydration, tired and shortened muscles, or an imbalance of electrolytes (mineral salts within the blood). By regularly stretching, drinking plenty of water, and maintaining a normal balance of electrolytes - possibly through vitamin and mineral supplementation- you should be able to avoid this problem.

Stitches

A stitch is a deep throbbing pain felt in the abdominal area which often causes sufferers to stop training. There is no single definite remedy for the cause or treatment of a stitch. The most popular theory is that they are caused by either drinking too much or eating a meal too close to running. This extra 'bounce' from the weight of food and drink in the stomach can cause a ligament which connects the stomach to the rib cage to go into spasm.

Whenever you move your body, the blood flow gets diverted to the working muscles instead of the internal organs. This means If you have just had a meal then there is not enough blood being sent to the digestive system to digest food which could also be a cause stomach problems.

Another theory is the diaphragm (the muscle that assists in breathing) can go into spasm due to fatigue. If you do get a stitch, try to hold your stomach in either by contracting the muscles or placing your hands over the area and squeezing, breathe using shallow breaths, slow down, and reduce the bounce in your stride. If none of these work, you may need to stop for a couple of minutes to give it time to wear off.

TREATING INJURIES

If you feel an increase in pain after an injury, you should stop because running through this pain will only slow down the recovery process or even make the injury more serious. A more sinister outcome is that by continuing to run and subconsciously protecting the injury by altering your natural running style, means a secondary injury may develop.

For any muscular tears, the usual form of action is abbreviated into the acronym RICE:

REST – Don't train for at least 24 – 28 hours; depending on the severity of the tea. Try not to use it at all for the immediate preceding hours.

ICE – Apply a bag of ice or frozen peas to the damaged area. This helps to constrict the capillaries which can reduce muscle bleeds.

Compression – Apply pressure to the area using a bandage or tying something around it. This can reduce swelling and bleeding.

Elevation – The idea behind this is to raise the damaged area above the level of the heart to reduce blood flow - thereby lessening bleeding and speeding up the healing process.

Any injury lasting more than a couple of weeks, or one that gets worse with subsequent runs, will require medical attention. Make an appointment to see a professional. It is important to see the right person as injuries can be misdiagnosed at times, which usually leads to much longer recovery times.

Physiotherapists, sports therapists, chiropractors, massage therapists, and osteopaths are all experts who should be approached for advice. Always check they hold current qualifications and - if possible- have been recommended to you by someone you know personally. Ask them to diagnose the problem and to give you advice on how to train, rest, and repair the area. Also, ask how long the injury could take to heal and how many visits you might need to make for treatment.

12 CHAPTER HOW TO **PREVENT INJURIES**

By following the instructions in this guide and increasing your distances very gradually, you should be able to avoid and prevent the most common of these injuries. Above all else, always listen to what your body is telling you. If you feel the first signs that something wrong, don't simply run through it. Stop to investigate it further. Unfortunately, the sad truth is, that many runners cause themselves serious long-term injury by continuing to work through seemingly small pains because of an unwillingness to stop or slow down.

The following points should give you an overview of the best ways to avoid suffering from injuries:

- Make slow and gradual changes when increasing the distance you are running.
- Make sure to alternate your training days and always take rest days.
- Spend some time and money choosing the correct type of footwear for your particular running style.
- Always listen to your body.
- Make sure you stretch regularly - both before and after your training.
- Include a thorough and gradual warm-up which includes a gentle increase in the heart rate, warmth of the muscles, then mobilising the joints and relevant stretches.
- Drink plenty of fluids daily.
- Avoid over-training.

- Try to train on a variety of different running surfaces. Road, grass, and dirt tracks are ideal for strengthening the deeper muscles of the lower body. However, you should ease into different surfaces gradually; for example, don't simply decide one day that you are going to run a long distance on an unusual surface. Instead, try much shorter runs at first and build up from there.
- If in doubt, consult your physiotherapist or doctor.

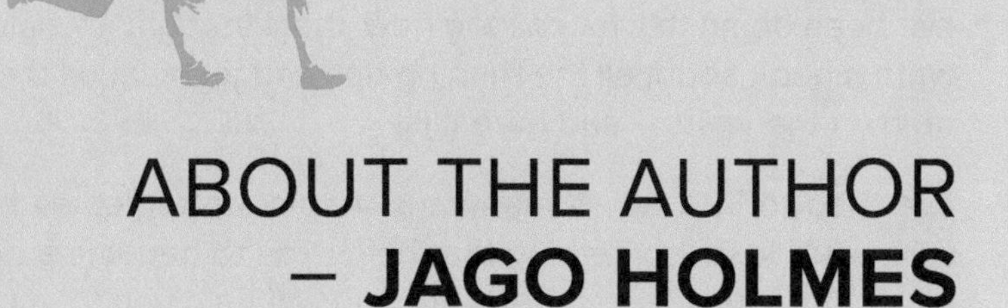

ABOUT THE AUTHOR – **JAGO HOLMES**

Please allow me to introduce myself. My name is Jago Holmes and I am the author and creator of '*Top Running Tips - 101 Ways To Improve Your Running.*'

I am also the owner and principal trainer here at New Image Personal Training in Halifax, UK. We regularly work with over 100 clients every week in our exclusive 1 :1 studios.

I am a fully qualified and experienced fitness trainer and running coach. My personal training company has been in operation for more than a decade now and we consistently get great results from our 1:1 clients and so I'd like to share my knowledge and success with you now.

I've written many newspaper and magazine articles for the local press and created a range of digital e-books and weight loss packages. I regularly present fat loss seminars as well as running my acclaimed '8 Week Weight Loss Challenge.'

I studied at the University of Leeds; completing my training with YMCA in 2000. After 3 years, I attained the YMCA Personal Trainer award - one of the highest and most respected qualifications available in the UK for Personal Trainers.

As a personal trainer I often work with clients who want to start running for a variety of reasons – to be more active, improve their fitness levels, join a running club, to enter a race... the list goes on!

I've been doing this for so long now, that I thought it would be great to write a book about all the running tips and techniques that I've picked up over the years – and here it is!

I've tried to include as many actionable strategies as I can and I'm sure you'll learn something that helps you to become a better runner. Many of the tips I've shared with you will help you to improve - if you incorporate them into your running program.

I've included tips that I learnt nearly a decade ago and some which I've only just recently discovered, so there's plenty for you to learn and use in your own running. I truly hope you enjoy reading this book. Please leave your positive comments for others to benefit from your experience, as it makes the Amazon marketplace a much more honest and enjoyable place for people to shop and buy books.

If you can think of any ways you feel this book could be improved, please send an email to me here – *jago@jagoholmes.com* and I'll try to add your suggestions.

OTHER BOOKS THAT MIGHT BE OF INTEREST TO YOU

Here are a couple of great recipe books which will help to keep you energised and feeling wonderful all day long. You'll discover loads of delicious recipes which are low in fat, easy to make and use relatively inexpensive ingredients. Click on the blue text links below to find out more and discover a wonderful collection of some of the tastiest salad and soups recipes around!

HEALTHY SOUPS

Healthy soups are one of the best ways to use a wide range of wholesome fresh meats and vegetables to create amazingly tasty and nutritious meals.

Whether you want a warming soup by the fireside on a cold and frosty winter's evening, or a refreshingly tangy and delicious midday snack to keep you going through until dinner in the summer, there's a perfect recipe in this soup cookbook for you:

http://www.amazon.com/Recipes-Quick-Delicious-Healthy-ebook/dp/B009B5GYN2

* * * *

HEALTHY SALADS

Preparing your own healthy food often means slaving away for hours; but most of the super quick salads and dressings in this book can be prepared and ready to eat in less than 10 minutes!

Another great thing about making your own salad is that it can be a very cheap meal for anyone cooking on a budget. Salads are no longer simply a summer dish, with some of the warm salads in this book you can also treat yourself to a healthy, warming and refreshing meal in the middle of winter:

http://www.amazon.com/Healthy-Prepare-Serve-Delicious-ebook/dp/B009FT4PFI

* * * *

WALKING FOR WEIGHT LOSS

Many people struggle to fit a time for exercise into their busy lifestyles- and it's an understandable problem. You've got to have time to spare. You need to get to the gym, get changed, do your workout, get showered and changed again and then travel back home. Depending on where you live and your work schedule, his could so easily take up a couple of hours of your precious time.

But there is a solution... Walking, but not walking as you know it!

Go here to find out more about a unique fat burning system you can start today -

http://www.amazon.com/Walking-For-Weight-Loss-ebook/dp/B0081KQ118

Thank you so much for reading my book, I really do hope that you've enjoyed reading it got something from my experience. Until technology comes up with a better way, the only way I have to get any feedback from my readers is through reviews.

So, I would be very grateful if you could take a minute to leave an honest review on Amazon (even if it is only a couple of words). I read all reviews and greatly appreciate the feedback.

Warmest regards!

Jago

Made in United States
Troutdale, OR
08/04/2023